# THE ROMAN CONQUEST
# OF BRITAIN

Graham Webster, MA, PhD, FSA, AMA, is Reader in
Romano-British Archaeology in the Department of
Extramural Studies at the University of Birmingham.
He was at one time Curator of the Grosvenor Museum,
Chester, and has written other books on Roman archae-
ology and excavation techniques, and many papers to
learned journals.

D. R. Dudley was Professor of Latin at the University of
Birmingham. Educated at King Edward's School, Birmingham, and St John's College, Oxford, he was also a
lecturer in Classics at Reading University and, from
1945–1955, Director of Extramural Studies at the University of Birmingham.

He wrote several books about ancient Rome and
Britain under the Romans, and contributed to many
newspapers and journals on the subjects.

Professor Dudley died in 1972.

## CONDITIONS OF SALE

*British Battles Series*

# THE ROMAN CONQUEST
# OF BRITAIN

## AD 43–57

### Graham Webster and Donald R. Dudley

**REVISED EDITION**

## PAN BOOKS LTD : LONDON

First published 1965 by B. T. Batsford Ltd
This revised edition published 1973 by Pan Books Ltd,
33 Tothill Street, London SW1


ISBN 0 330 23772 1

*Printed and Bound in England by*
*Hazell Watson & Viney Ltd*
*Aylesbury, Bucks*

# Contents

# List of Illustrations

(between pages 100 and 101)

# Acknowledgements

The authors and publishers wish to thank the following for the illustrations appearing in this book :

Aerofilms and Aero Pictorial Ltd for plates 8 and 10; Musée Calvet, Avignon for plate 3; the Trustees of the British Museum for plate 12; Colchester and Essex Museum for plates 2 and 4; Dorset County Museum for plate 11; Altertumsmuseum, Mainz for plate 5; Mansell Collection for plate 1; Helga Schmidt-Glassner for plate 7; Kunsthistorisches Museum, Vienna for plate 13; The National Museum of Wales for plates 6 and 15.

## NOTE

The italicized numerals in the text, placed in parentheses, refer to the plate numbers.

## Preface to the First Edition

It was with some misgiving that we accepted the publisher's invitation to contribute to the series on British Battles a book about the Claudian Invasion of Britain. The battles with which we shall have to deal are neither uninteresting nor unimportant; after all, they determined the history of this island for more than three centuries. But the evidence at our command is of an altogether different nature from that available to the modern military historian. He has official dispatches, the reports of war-correspondents, maps, battle-plans, films, photographs, and private accounts and diaries in almost embarrassing profusion and detail. For example, in the account of the Alma, in a companion volume, we read that 'his [Sir George Brown's] contribution to the battle had so far been nil, but he was reputed to have been the only man in the army to have shaved that morning'. Again: 'only when this had been done to the satisfaction of Colonel Mauleverer of the 30th did he resume his place in the line and was heard unconcernedly asking Major Patullo for a light for his cigar'. Such particularity is not for the historian of the Claudian Invasion.

But our problems go deeper. We have two major battles, neither of which can be placed on the map with absolute confidence. The lines of the Roman advance to the Severn, the Humber, and the Exe are known only in the most general way, even if their terminal points are fairly certain. At a later phase, forts and military roads impose a more reliable geographical pattern; we are better informed of the way in which the Romans consolidated their conquests in Britain than that by which they were won. As all who have tried it know too well, there is a fundamental difficulty about trying to combine the two kinds of evidence we have – that of the scanty historical texts and that of archaeology. The two sort ill together : the narrative of battles should move fast, the evidence of archaeology must be presented in detailed and sometimes tedious argument. Some of this we have tried to reserve for the Appendices and Notes, hoping thus to provide a fairly unencumbered text for those whose interest is rather in military history than in Roman Britain. Even so, we fear this book will be an awkward recruit when it comes to stand in line with Balaclava and Malplaquet, with Waterloo and El Alamein.

We have to acknowledge help and advice from many sources, and notably from Lady Aileen Fox, Professor Eric Birley, Mr Leo Rivet, Dr Michael Jarrett, Mr R. F. Jessup, and Mr Arnold Baker. Professor Harry Thorpe, Dr John Wilkes and Mr Anthony Birley, our colleagues in Birmingham, have given us the benefit of expert knowledge on several points. Our thanks are also due to Mr Frederick Reed for reading the text and indicating ambiguities, and to Mrs Muriel Stanley for undertaking the arduous task of compiling the index. If we have still contrived to make mistakes, they are entirely our own.

*Birmingham, 1964*

G.W.
D.R.D.

# Preface to the Second Edition

It has been a melancholy task preparing this edition, since I have been without the support of my colleague Professor D. R. Dudley, who died in 1972. Fortunately, little of his contribution has required amendment; the main changes are due to the considerable amount of new archaeological evidence which has come to light through aerial reconnaissance, excavations and casual finds. In trying to bring the situation up to date, I owe much to my co-workers in the field for allowing me to make use of their discoveries, often before they have had the opportunity to publish. I have attempted summaries in the intervening period ('The Claudian Frontiers in Britain', *Studien zu den Militärgrenzen Roms*, 1967, 42–53, and 'The Military Situations in Britain between AD 43 and 71', *Britannia*, i (1970), 179–197, and we also now have the revised edition of the invaluable *The Roman Frontiers in Wales*, 1969, by V. E. Nash-Williams, edited by Michael G. Jarrett. But every year brings its new crop of finds and ideas and the whole study remains in a fluid state. In considering the archaeological evidence this new edition must be considered as a report of work in hand.

*Birmingham, 1973*                                            G.W.

# 1 Roman Preparations

I

Early in the spring of AD 43, the coast of Gaul opposite the chalk cliffs of Britain was the scene of great activity. A vast array of troops and horses had been gradually assembling since the end of winter. From all the small harbours along the coast, ships were being sailed or towed to the port of embarkation. In the shipyards swarms of workmen were busy repairing and building new craft. Along the new roads to the Channel ports trundled the waggons loaded with stores and equipment from every part of Gaul. Plans were well advanced for the Great Invasion. The Emperor Claudius, two years on the throne and in his early fifties, saw an opportunity for gaining a triumph in Britain which would round off the distinguished achievements of his kinsmen, Drusus and Germanicus, and of himself, in the north-western provinces.

Much care had been taken in selecting the high command and staff, as was usual in the reign of Claudius. The commander-in-chief was Aulus Plautius, who was connected with the Emperor through his kinswoman Plautia Urgulanilla, Claudius' first wife. One of the most distinguished

senators of the day, Plautius had held the consulship in AD
29, and was governor of Pannonia at the time of his appointment to the British expedition. There he would have had
experience of a warlike frontier, though we can give no
details of his military career. His task must have been to
supervise the assembly of the expeditionary force, conduct it
across the Channel, and command at least the first phases of
military operations, depending on the degree of British resistance encountered. He would then become Governor of
Britain, and organize that part of it selected for development as a Roman province. Among the legionary commanders was the future Emperor Vespasian, then in charge
of the IInd *Augusta* and with his service honours to come,
and accompanied by his older brother Flavius Sabinus.
Another senior commander was Hosidius Geta, who had so
recently distinguished himself in Mauretania.[1] The size and
composition of the expeditionary force had been carefully
considered, bearing in mind the lessons learned from the
campaigns of Julius Caesar. Caesar had taken two legions
and an unstated number of cavalry on his first invasion in
55 BC; five legions 'and an equal force of cavalry' on the
second in 54 BC.[2] Careful attention had been given to the
cavalry force for the Claudian expedition and an unusual
command, that of *praefectus equitatus*, assigned to Didius
Gallus, the third governor of Britain (AD 52–58?).[3] Four
legions were assigned for the operations of Aulus Plautius,
perhaps with detachments from others, although participa-
tion by the VIIIth Legion has recently been challenged,[4]
and the number of auxiliaries would have brought the force
up to 40–50,000 men.

The Rhine command had allocated three legions for the
invasion : the IInd *Augusta* from Argentoratum (Stras-
bourg), the XXth *Valeria* from Novaesium (Neuss), the
XIV *Gemina* from Moguntiacum (Mainz). The remaining
legion of the force came from the Danube command, probably from Siscia (Sisak) in Pannonia.[5] This was the IXth
*Hispana*, and it probably made the long journey of more

than a thousand miles as escort to the commander-in-chief. All were legions with experience of warfare in Northern Europe. The IInd, raised by Augustus, had served in Spain, but was moved to Germany in AD 10. The IXth had also been in Spain, before its transfer to the Danube some time earlier than AD 6. The XIVth, another Augustan legion, which was to distinguish itself in Britain, had served in Illyricum and Germany. The XXth had served under Tiberius in the Pannonian rebellion, after which it was sent to the Rhine. The auxiliary units included men from Gaul, Thrace and Germany : the presence of Batavian troops who were experts in river-crossings is especially notable.[6]

So far, the Roman staff-work had been of a high order. But battles are won, in part, in soldiers' minds, and for this great enterprise the psychological preparation had been less than thorough. This showed itself when, preparations complete, the order was given to embark. Suddenly the commanders discovered the baleful influence of the Ocean, and the almost pathological dread it aroused in the invasion force. This sprang from many causes. To the geographers of the Greek and Roman world Britain was a monstrous aberration – quite literally, it ought not to be there. It could be shown by reason that the habitable world was bounded on all sides by the Ocean, and that no lands or islands lay beyond. Except for the British Isles, and they – against all the rules – contained the largest island known to Roman science![7] It was wrong; Britain, although (regrettably) it existed, must form 'another world' (*alter orbis*). So the geographers. But, to the superstitious soldiers, Britain was a land of mystery. Travellers' tales went round the camps, and lost nothing in the telling. The legions from Germany had grim experience of the hazards of warfare in northern waters. Few passages of Tacitus are more dramatic than the account of the great surge of the North Sea that trapped and wrecked the expeditionary force of Germanicus between the mouths of the Ems and the Rhine in the autumn of AD 16.[8] A few survivors of the storm-battered Roman Fleet were swept across

to Britain and later returned by the island chiefs. 'Not a
man,' says Tacitus, 'returned from a distance without his
story of marvels – terrible hurricanes, unknown birds, sea-
monsters, creatures half-human and half-bestial – all of
which they had seen, or believed in their fear.' More soberly,
the historian adds his own comment '. . . that Ocean is more
stormy than any of the other seas of the world'. For a Roman
force to cross the Channel and invade Britain meant the
shattering of barriers that were as much psychological as
physical. They had been too strong for the force assembled
by the megalomaniac Emperor Gaius, three or four years
earlier, though what truth lies behind the strange tale recorded by the historians on that occasion we do not know.
Certainly Gaius was forced to call off the invasion, the only
achievement of which was the building of a lighthouse at
Boulogne.

And now the troops of Claudius, agog with wild rumour
and knowing that the previous expedition had never sailed,
refused to embark.[9] It was a critical moment for the military
commander. The troops could hardly be treated with the
harsh discipline usual for desertion or cowardice in the face
of the enemy. A bold and imaginative commander might
have won them over by his force of personality, but Aulus
Plautius was not such a man. He was at a disadvantage in
that three of his four legions were from the Rhine command,
and he had had little time to enforce his authority over them.
Perhaps, too, he did not understand how deep-seated was
their dread of the unknown island. So he played for safety,
and spread his responsibility by appealing for guidance from
the Emperor. A confidential agent was sent in the person of
Narcissus, an Imperial freedman, and the story goes that the
soldiers were at first enraged that a man who had previously
been a slave should deign to address them, mounted on the
tribunal of the commander-in-chief. But the comic irony of
the situation struck them and their contempt turned to deri-
sion and to shouts of '*io Saturnalia*'; for at the Saturnalia the
slaves wore their masters' costumes and gave the orders. The

real state of affairs in the administration of Claudius had not penetrated to the army camps along the Rhine. For the freedmen did give the orders, and Narcissus may well have played a part in the planning of the British expedition. Having thus worked off their bad humour, the troops quietly embarked. These are obviously the very bare bones of a strange story. Narcissus must have been a highly intelligent and able man to have been selected for the post he held, equivalent to a Permanent Secretary. No doubt a clever Greek might use subtle methods on the Romans with their stolid outlook. His oration, with its calculated broad humour, may have been the final stage in a complex process of restoring morale and removing doubts and difficulties provoked by the invasion.

But the result of the near-mutiny was a serious delay, and Dio Cassius says it made the Roman departure late in the season.[10] Although it is not specifically stated, it would seem from this that Narcissus was sent by Claudius from Rome. An Imperial courier service had been established by Augustus and staging-posts were available along all the main roads, maintained by the local authorities through whose district they passed. Some very fast times are on record for emergencies, but the couriers used four-wheeled enclosed carts and achieved an average speed of about five miles an hour. On special occasions relays of gallopers could maintain an average of ten miles an hour day and night.[11] It is thus hardly likely that the messenger sent by Plautius would have taken less than five days to reach Massilia, where he would have embarked for Rome, adding another three to six days to the voyage. Narcissus, on the other hand, an important state official, would not have proceeded at this rate, but with a large train of attendants would have taken two or three times as long. From the time Plautius dispatched his messenger to the arrival of Narcissus may have been up to two months, and it was probably well into July before the fleet sailed.

II

Before we follow the armada across the Channel, digressions must be made to consider in brief, the organization and equipment of the Roman Army and its opponents, and, secondly, the lessons that had been learned on both sides from the invasions of Julius Caesar.

The Praetorians, or Imperial Bodyguard, a *corps d'élite*, only took the field when led by the Emperor in person. They were normally based on Rome. The legions formed the backbone of the army, and there were then twenty-seven of these formations. They were tough, well-trained, disciplined infantry, made up of Roman citizens. Recruitment in the west was limited at this time to Italy, Spain and Gaul and the Roman *coloniae*. There were still in the legions many men from Italy itself, although gradually the extension of the franchise and the foundation of *coloniae* introduced more and more men from the outer regions of the Roman world. A legion was composed of ten cohorts, each of 480 men, except the first, which was double that number. The cohorts consisted of six centuries of eighty men. Attached to the legion was a small body of horsemen whose main duties were those of dispatch riders and guards; they could not be regarded as an effective cavalry force. At this period the emphasis was on the foot soldier who bore the brunt of the fighting; the use of cavalry as shock troops came only later. There were also many specialists – clerks for stores and records, armourers and blacksmiths, master stone-masons and carpenters, artificers of all kinds, and of course medical staff. The legion had its own architect and water engineer but these, like doctors and surgeons, were regarded merely as technicians.

The legionaries were uniformly equipped with body armour which at this time may have been undergoing a change. The jerkin of hardened leather reinforced with metal plates was being replaced by the more complicated strip armour (*lorica segmentata*). This is seen in its fully developed form on Trajan's Column (*16*). There are back and front plates giving protection up to the neck, and over these are the curved overlapping steel strips, hinged at the back and fastened with thongs laced into hooks at the front. To give flexibility of movement the strips had to slide one over the other, for had they been fastened separately to the jerkin below they would have had the effect of a steel corset. In the scenes from the Column, the armoured soldiers are shown in many postures, engaged in strenuous activities which demand complete freedom. This armour came only as far as the hips : below this the only protection was from the apron made of leather and bronze strips hanging from the belt, which swung sporran like between the legs without interfering with movement. The helmet was a well-designed piece of equipment : like the *lorica* it was going through a phase of development at this period. The older type was like a jockey cap with bronze dome and a horizonal projection at the back; only the brow-ridge gave protection at the front, apart from the pair of hinged cheek-pieces. This simple robust bronze helmet was being replaced by a composite form with an iron skull cap, the main difference being the deeper protection at the back of the neck, where lay the great weakness of the other type. The legionary shield was of a large semi-cylindrical type, which when held close to the body gave protection from the chin to the thigh along the whole of one side. In spite of its size it was probably fairly light, being made of a kind of plywood; it was bound only at the edges in metal and had a strong bronze central boss for the internal hand-grip. The outer surface was covered with red leather, on which there were gilded bronze patterns representing the thunderbolts of Jupiter. On the march, the soldiers carried their shields by a strap over the head so that they hung down the left side : they were held only in battle conditions. The arm slid through a leather loop so that the main weight of the shield rested on the forearm rather than the hand itself.

The attacking weapons were the javelin (*pilum*) and the short sword (*gladius*). The wooden *pilum* was seven foot long with an iron shank having a hardened point. Each legionary carried two of these; they were thrown in volleys from distances of about forty and thirty yards. They were not so much for killing as for disarming the enemy. The hard point pierced the enemy shield held up in defence and the shank bent under the weight of the *pilum*. It could not be easily withdrawn, so that the shield had to be discarded. The legionaries then drew their short swords and engaged the enemy in close work, with the great defensive advantage – as compared with a barbarian enemy – of having large close-fitting shields and body armour. The sword was used for stabbing, like the modern bayonet. The Celts were used to open warfare where they could swing their long swords against individual targets. The Roman legionaries were trained to fight in close formation and pressed constantly on the enemy in a tight mêlée, where the short sword could be used more effectively. The long, curved Roman shield was useful in protecting the left side when held close; in the attack it could be thrust forward to knock the enemy off balance and so provide a target for the sword. This was used with an upward jab and plenty of wrist action. The Celtic method of fighting was based on individual combat, and against their warriors the close assault of legionaries in their tight formations proved most effective. The Romans had another great advantage in the training of their units. The Celts could be heroic fighters under inspired leadership, but they had no effective organization; once the battle was joined it was difficult to direct and manoeuvre particular sections. With the Roman organization this was no obstacle. With prearranged signals given by trumpets or bugles, centuries or cohorts could be disengaged, and the direction of attack turned as weaknesses in the enemy line were found and exploited.

While the main frontal assaults were delivered by the legionaries, another branch of the army, the *auxilia*, played their part, on the flanks. As their name implies, these troops

were first regarded as aids to the legions. They were re-
cruited originally from barbarian tribes and retained their
names and methods of fighting. While at first in pre-Augus-
tan days they were sometimes an ill-organized rabble of locals
liable to desert at a critical moment, they later became an
integral part of the Roman Army. Augustus, with his
peculiar genius, rationalized the situation by gradually turning them into a permanent force. They were levied from
almost every province of the Roman Empire except Achaea
(Greece), and in special cases this levy was preferred to
tribute or requisitions of other kinds. In the late Republic,
citizenship had been conferred on certain units for outstanding services, but it may have been Claudius who made this
important provision for all auxiliaries who completed an
honourable period of service. There was thus an incentive
to join this branch of the army, and its total effect over the
first two centuries of Imperial rule in extending the franchise
must have been very considerable. By the end of the first
century AD there may have been as many as 200,000 auxiliaries in the army. As each served twenty-five years there
would thus (allowing for casualties) have been five or six
thousand new citizens every year; add to this the wives and
children, and over the first two centuries, at a modest estimate, the total may well have been up to five million new
citizens through this source alone. At this period all the units
were of cohort strength, ie about five hundred men. There
were basically three types of unit,[12] the cavalry *ala*, the part-
mounted unit and the infantry cohort, in that order of status.
The number of units raised varied with the population in
each province. Thus there were (about AD 100) at least
thirty-two cohorts of Gauls, thirteen of Britons, nine of
Batavians, fifteen of Raetians, eight of Dalmatians, six of
Asturians, thirty-nine from Gallia Belgica (including the
two Germanies) and sixty from Spain, while there were at
least eight Thracian cavalry *alae*, upwards of twenty from
Gaul, one *ala* of *Dromedarii*, and so on. Each group of units
so raised would have been organized in the same manner,

but equipped in their native style. In this way the army had troops with a great variety of specialist experience. The infantry might be lightly armed and mobile with throwing spear, or heavily armed and static, with a heavy spear like a pike to break up a cavalry charge. There were several kinds of missile users, from archers to slingers and stone-throwers. Cavalry likewise varied in their armour and weapons. One has only to study the great variety of spears, lances and javelins found on Roman military sites to appreciate their complexity.

One of the important aspects of the army from the archaeologist's point of view is that of their forts and camps, since it is from the excavation of these that much of our information is obtained. When the army was campaigning in Gaul under Caesar in the first century BC, the troops were always housed in tents. There is no indication of a permanent fort with buildings. During the winter, army groups were settled down in a selected area in their *hiberna*, but even these still lived in tents. In the summer campaigns the army always constructed a fortified camp for the night; the tents were set out in an orderly array on a carefully constructed grid pattern, the unit being organized in strict order of seniority round the central tent which housed the commander and his staff. The streets or through-ways were of particular importance for the rapid assembly of horses and men at any danger point. There is an interesting passage in which Caesar relates how he deliberately reduced the size of a fort by cutting down the width of the roads in order to deceive the Gauls as to the size of the force. This suggests a degree of standardization by which the enemy could estimate with reasonable accuracy the size of the Roman army facing them by the area of their camps. Under normal circumstances, when an army was on the march, the defences of most camps consisted of a ditch only about a yard wide and deep. The bank on the inside was made of stacked turves, to which was added the spoil from the ditch; on to the top were fixed the palisade stakes (*pila muralia*), each about seven feet long. Each man was allocated two of these stakes, and from this it can be estimated that they would be about six inches apart in the bank, and tied together at the centre. The result was an adequate fence to keep stray animals out, and soldiers with a tendency to wander, inside the camp, but against a serious attack these defences were not very formidable. The Roman Army was at this period an attacking force and these camps were not intended to withstand sieges; it was much more effective to engage the enemy in the open. There were occasions, however, when it was necessary to dig in. This is illustrated by another episode from Caesar when he needed to deceive the Gauls by pretending to be afraid. The legionaries were ordered to raise the height of the ramparts and block the gateways with turves and then withdraw men from the ramparts. The Gauls thought the gates would be the most strongly held points, so they began to fill in the ditches and pull down the bank beyond; while they were so engaged the Romans slipped out of the rear gates and attacked them so unexpectedly that the Gauls, although in some strength, were put to flight. It is clear from this that in some cases mere tented enclosures could have considerable defences. This seems to be true of Britain. The larger fort at Metchley in Birmingham has a double ditch and large rampart, but no sign of permanent buildings within. Evidence from Waddon Hill in Dorset also suggests that the defences were first erected by quarrying the hill-top, just as the Britons did for their hill-forts; only later was the interior levelled out and the quarry pits filled in for the erection of timber buildings.

In contrast to the camps, perhaps better referred to as marching camps, are the permanent forts with their timber barracks and other buildings. Here the unit settled down in a position for an indefinite period. It was between the period of Caesar and Claudius that the idea of the permanent fort came into being. Along the Rhine and Danube frontiers the army gradually consolidated and in the hard winters the tented quarters would have been a source of grievance to the soldiers. Although this grievance was not stressed during the mutinies on the Rhine under Tiberius, it is clear that a change of policy was desirable. By the time Britain was invaded, the men could expect to be provided with permanent buildings, having timber and clay walls to keep out the wind, rain and snow. These buildings at first were laid out like tents; only by the Flavian period was their internal planning rationalized into a stereotyped text-book pattern. Much later most of the principal buildings were built of stone, and with this comes also the inscription in permanent form. Whereas from the northern garrisons there is a great mass of epigraphic material from which it is possible to learn many details of chronology and of the names of units, in the first century these inscriptions would have been carved on wood panels, and none survive.[13] Archaeological evidence for dating is thus confined to a study of coins, pottery, brooches, and similar objects which may by their changes of fashion yield such information.

The third branch of the Roman Army was the fleet.[14] There is little doubt that at this period its organization was flexible and varied according to circumstances. Basically it was not considered as a fighting arm and thus was ranked as inferior to the *auxilia*. The main duties of the fleet were to transport troops and stores across the seas and over large rivers where a bridge was impracticable. Light ships were also invaluable for reconnaissance and communications. There had been many occasions during the civil wars on which Augustus was left in no doubt as to the value of sea power in securing the routes which controlled main supplies. It was Agrippa who became in effect the architect of the Imperial Navy with the establishment of the first permanent naval base at Fréjus (Forum Iulii); later Augustus built bases in Italy at Misenum and Ravenna. As the needs of the Empire grew, so the fleet began to proliferate, and new squadrons were raised. The *classis Moesica* was formed to patrol the lower Danube, the *classis Pannonica* the upper Danube, the Save and the Drave, and the *classis Pontica* the

Black Sea. Clearly the lower Rhine would have needed a squadron, and this was created by Drusus the Elder, who had a canal cut between the Rhine and the Zuyder Zee to make a more direct contact with the North Sea. The conquest of Britain demanded a large force of transports. This in effect created the *classis Britannica*; there is evidence that skilled personnel were drafted from the Mediterranean. Once formed it became a permanent institution, and one finds along the south-east coast tiles stamped 'CL BR'. The internal organization of the squadron with its many different kinds of ships, specialist shore officers, and craftsmen, made it the most complex branch of the whole army. As the recruitment at the end of the Republic was largely from the eastern Mediterranean, it is hardly surprising to find many of the titles were Greek, such as *trierarchus* and *navarchus*.

It would be interesting to know more about the ships of the British squadron. The war galleys designed for Mediterranean waters were notoriously unstable and, as Caesar discovered, much stouter ships were needed for the difficult waters of the Channel and the North Sea. That this problem must have been overcome is clearly demonstrated by the use made by Agricola of a squadron to circumnavigate the north coast of Britain. Perhaps the ships of the Veneti, whose ocean-going qualities showed up well in Caesar's Gallic and British campaigns, may have served as a model. How carefully the Romans of this period studied local conditions in constructing their transport vessels is seen in Tacitus' account of the preparations for Germanicus' expedition of AD 16.[15]

A thousand ships were thought to be adequate, and their construction was pushed ahead. Some were of shallow draught, pointed bow and stern, and broad-beamed to withstand heavy seas. Others were flat-bottomed to allow grounding. Most of them were equipped with steering-oars on both sides, to allow of quick movement forwards and backwards. Many had decks for the transport of artillery, horses and supplies. They were easy to sail, their oars gave them a turn of speed, and the keenness of their complement made them impressive and formidable.

### III

What kind of opposition could the Roman Army expect to meet in Britain? The Belgic peoples of Britain, against whom they were soon to be engaged, were much akin to the Gauls and fought in the same manner. Body armour in the form of helmets and breast-plates was too expensive for any but the chiefs, their families, and their immediate entourage. The poorer Britons of the rank and file had little if any protection and, as Caesar relates, placed their reliance on magic. They painted their bodies with blue woad, probably in intricate patterns of curvilinear designs like the tattoo used by many primitive peoples today. The object was not only to provide protection through sacred symbols and ritual, but also by their very appearance to strike terror into their opponents. Since Caesar's day the Britons may have been softened by the introduction of luxury goods from the Roman world, but there had probably been much fighting in the conquests of Cunobelinus. Plautius could not expect an easy victory over tribesmen lured into a more civilized way of life. The Britons still put their faith in an instrument of war that had long been abandoned elsewhere – the chariot. The popular view of this vehicle is seen in the 'Boadicea' statue on the Embankment, where the British queen is shown riding in a solid-looking cart similar to those still seen on roundabouts at fun fairs. The Celtic chariot was quite different, and the way in which it was used is vividly portrayed by Caesar. He had first seen British chariots in action during the first invasion, and showed interest in this unusual method of warfare by giving a brief description of its technique :

In chariot fighting the Britons begin by driving all over the field hurling javelins, and generally the terror inspired by the horses and the noise of the wheels is sufficient to throw their opponents' ranks into disorder. Then, after making their way between the squadrons of their own cavalry, they jump down from the chariots and engage on foot. In the meantime their charioteers retire a short distance from the battle and place the chariots in such a position that their masters, if hard pressed by numbers, have an easy means of retreat to their own lines. Thus they combine the mobility of cavalry with the staying-power of infantry, and by daily training and practice they attain such proficiency that even on a steep incline they are able to control the horses at full gallop, and to check them in a moment. They can run along the chariot pole, stand on the yoke, and get back into the chariot as quick as lightning.'[16]

The vehicle suitable for these rapid manoeuvres would need to be very light and open at both ends. If more of the Arch of Claudius had survived there is little doubt that it would have shown examples among the trophies. Reconstruction has only been possible through the discovery of pieces of metalwork such as the wheels, hub caps, and other fittings. Some of these, found in Anglesey during the last war,[17] enabled Sir Cyril Fox to attempt a convincing reconstruction,[18] and a model of this can now be seen in the National Museum of Wales (6). It is a small square vehicle with wicker-work sides open at both ends to allow the warrior either to leap out at the back or run along the pole to the front and engage the enemy in single combat. This is, essentially, a kind of fighting designed for the aristocratic warrior. Fast streams of chariots could move swiftly along an unprotected flank, sting it with volleys of javelins, and escape before pursuit could be mounted. The chariots could also bring the warriors rapidly to any part of the battle needing their aid. The warriors would run out on foot, drive back the foe, and then retire to their vehicles, to be removed from the scene with speed and efficiency. It was ideal for open warfare where the heroic swordsman could show his prowess; against the Romans it could never be more than a novelty and annoyance.

IV

It can be no part of the plan of this book to narrate the details of Caesar's two British expeditions : still less,[19] to re-open any of the unsolved problems which they present. They concern us only for purposes of comparison. In AD 43, what lessons did they contain for Roman invaders and British defenders? And what light does their history throw for us on the diplomatic and military events of almost a century later than Caesar? These expeditions can, of course, only be understood in their context. It has been pointed out how they fall into place with Pompey's campaigns against the peoples of the Caucasus, and with Caesar's own crossing of the Rhine in that same summer of 55 BC, to impress the tribes of western Germany with the power and reach of Rome. All derive from a technique for dealing with peoples on the fringe of the Empire, which might or might not lead to annexation as the next stage.[20] That personal reasons as well as public policy prompted Caesar in the British invasion of 55 BC is not to be doubted.[21] He believed Gaul to be pacified : yet he needed to justify the extension of his military command which he had gained at the Conference of Luca in 56 BC. On the other hand, Caesar had just been engaged in a great struggle with the Belgic peoples of Gaul; he knew that they had kinsmen in Britain, and knew, or at least claimed to know, that support, moral and direct, had been sent to Gaul by these people for use against him. Yet he could get virtually no information about Britain of the kind a Roman governor of Gaul would need to know. The Gaulish merchants, assembled for interrogation, could or would disclose nothing. And Caesar himself had all but wiped out the Veneti, who had for so long been the most active in the British trade.

So it is that the British invasion of 55 BC is presented by

Caesar as a reconnaissance in force. There was, even so, a preliminary phase of diplomacy, but the Kentish tribes learned of his plans and sent delegates to promise submission – no doubt in the hope of persuading him to call off the invasion. Caesar – well informed by now of barbarian psychology – merely told them to persist with this admirable intention, and to confirm it by sending hostages. Then he sent them back to Britain, accompanied by his own diplomatic agent, Commius, King of the Atrebates. Commius, at this stage a faithful friend of Caesar's, yet a man of authority on either side of the Channel, played a vital role in both expeditions. Meanwhile Caesar had sent out Gaius Volusenus on a warship to collect what military information he could. That officer did not succeed in landing in Britain, but by offshore observation presumably surveyed the coast for some distance on either side of Dover.

The start was delayed, and it was not until 25 August that Caesar sailed from Boulogne with the VIIth and Xth Legions. The cavalry were to embark separately, probably from Ambleteuse; in the event storms prevented them from ever landing in Britain, a damaging blow to the success of the whole operation. The Kentish chiefs, having failed to forestall invasion, now decided to oppose it. Their forces, occupying strong positions on the heights above Dover, looked so menacing that Caesar moved north-east along the coast, to find an open beach between Walmer Castle and Deal. Even so, it was an awkward landing-place in the face of opposition. The ships could not put in close ashore; there were no landing-craft; the legionaries were understandably nervous about leaping into the sea and wading ashore through enemy fire. Only the famous standard-bearer of the Xth (fit comrade of that American sergeant on the Argonne – 'Come on, do you want to live for ever?'), only he, and the effective use of Roman artillery from the ships, managed to get the troops to land. Once the legionaries were on the beach and able to draw up in battle-order, the Britons were routed, but lack of cavalry prevented any effective pursuit.

Again British policy changed; there was renewed talk of submission and hostages; preparations were made for a meeting between Caesar and the chiefs. This edifying event never took place. The moon was full and the spring tides were due : they coincided with the great storm that had blown the cavalry transports back to Gaul. The consequences for Caesar's ships – warships and transports alike – were disastrous. Twelve out of rather more than seventy were a total loss, others were waterlogged or badly damaged. Caesar's force was now on an enemy shore without transport or supplies.

Troops should not be in such a position, and good commanders do not put them there. It was the hour of opportunity for the Britons and they did not fail to take it. A party of the VIIth Legion, out to forage corn, fell into a cleverly baited trap and was very roughly handled by that combination of cavalry and chariot-fighting that the Britons employed with such skill. Only Caesar's intervention saved them, and even he could do no more than escort them back to camp. A few days later a major British assault was delivered on the camp itself. It was beaten off by the legionaries, but again there was no pursuit. By now the autumn equinox was near and Caesar was anxious to be gone : all the Britons wanted was to have him out. It suited both sides to talk peace and arrange for hostages – no need actually to deliver them. As soon as the weather turned fair, Caesar was off; those few fine autumn days were the only piece of good luck that came his way on this first expedition to Britain. Before a critical audience, in Gaul and Britain, his tactics had been ill-conceived in plan and slap-dash in execution. A blot had been made on his military reputation that would have to be erased. As for the Kentish chiefs, they could pass a happy winter, if they did not choose to look too far ahead. They had seen off the greatest Roman commander of his day. At one reaction, at least, we do not have to guess. For this mishandled affair the Roman Senate decreed a public thanksgiving for the unprecedented period of twenty days. The name of Mafeking is a reminder of the hysteria that can greet a military exploit of no great significance; again, the resolution of the Senate may, in part, be no more than a tribute to the efficiency of Caesar's political agents. But it also reflects, unmistakably, the Roman feeling about the remoteness of Britain, of the unknown hazards of the Ocean, and of the audacity of a commander who could dare this great military adventure.

The expedition of 54 BC was an altogether different story. Caesar took an adequate force – five legions, and 2,000 cavalry. He left in early July, with plenty of time for campaigning. But the storms of the great Gallic uprising were gathering, and he had to leave a further three legions and 2,000 cavalry to guard Boulogne and his communications with Rome; he also took to Britain a large number of Gallic nobles as hostages. He had got together an enormous fleet – more than 800 vessels of all descriptions, including many of his own design for conditions in the Channel. But he had made no effort to find a better landing-place than last year; indeed, south-westerly winds carried him up towards the North Foreland, and he had a hard row back with the tide to reach the open beaches a little north of his intended point, probably between Sandown Castle and Sandwich. This time there was no contested landing – the mere sight of the great Roman fleet had overawed the British forces and caused them to disperse. Once ashore, Caesar acted with the speed that brought him so many victories : leaving only ten cohorts to guard the beach-head and the ships he made a night march towards the Stour, where he knew the Britons were concentrated in force. British cavalry and charioteers disputed the Stour crossing in a battle shortly after dawn; they then fell back to the *oppidum* of Bigbury, which was to fall to the assault of the VIIth Legion by late afternoon. But before he had been on British soid for forty-eight hours, Caesar was made aware of the horrors of British weather. A great storm arose on the second night of the invasion, causing havoc to the Roman fleet, and wrecking, this time, forty ships. Ten days' work, carried on by night and day, was needed to beach the ships, carry out repairs, and extend the fortifications of the base-camp to enclose them. In the meantime, the military position on the British side had changed. The Kentish tribes had entrusted their cause to Cassivellaunus, chief of the Catuvellauni, whose capital was perhaps at Wheathampstead, near St Albans. (They may, indeed, have done this earlier, but Caesar did not find it out until the next stage of the campaign.) From this point a rational and effective strategy begins to make itself felt on the British side. When Caesar was once more able to drive inland, the enemy were ready to meet him on the Stour positions. British cavalry and charioteers, skilfully combined, harassed the Roman cavalry on the march. In a brisk action fought outside the Roman camp they impressed Caesar with their mobility and dash. The next day saw three legions and all the Roman cavalry in action on ground chosen by Caesar : this time the Roman cavalry finally swept the Britons from the field with heavy loss. Caesar is at pains to note that this was the last time Cassivellaunus was able to meet him in full strength. The passage implies, though it does not state, that Cassivellaunus commanded the British confederacy in person in these encounters. Though not victorious, he had other cards to play. The first was to dispute the passage of the Thames. What Caesar calls the only possible ford (Brentford? Coway Stakes?) had been protected on the north bank by *chevaux-de-frise* of sharp stakes, above and below water. A large British force was ready to engage beyond this barrier. But a force of Roman cavalry got across upstream, and the legionaries waded the river and advanced with such *élan* that the Britons fell into the panic that overtakes those whose trusted line of defence has failed. Cassivellaunus now turned to guerrilla tactics, dismissing all his forces except for 4,000 charioteers, harassing the Roman line of march, driving away cattle and destroying supplies. He was thus able to restrict Caesar's movements, but not to prevent him from reaching Wheathampstead.

This massive earthwork has been confidently claimed as the stronghold of Cassivellaunus by its discoverer, Sir Mortimer Wheeler.[22] It lies near Verulamium, which became the capital of the Catuvellauni before the move to Camulodunum, and this fact alone makes the claim more than possible. The only other candidate is the Belgic *oppidum* at Gatesbury, some ten miles to the north-east, unless there are other sites of this nature awaiting discovery elsewhere in Hertfordshire. There is no conclusive proof to link Cassivellaunus and Caesar with Wheathampstead, but its situation, extremely large defences, and enormous size, all make the suggestion most plausible. At one point on the west side the defence ditch is over a hundred feet across, and, although the boundary of the fortress on the north side has yet to be defined, the *oppidum* could extend over as much as a hundred acres. The pottery found in the excavations would also fit this period; and, as Sir Mortimer has indicated, the Belgae were the first people to penetrate this area, which must for prehistoric settlement be classed as marginal land, difficult to clear and cultivate without the iron tools of quantity and quality introduced into Britain by these new immigrants. It is significant that Cassivellaunus was successful in drawing the Roman army into this difficult country and continually harassing it without Caesar discovering the existence or site of the *oppidum*. It was not until he had this vital information from the emissaries of the Trinovantes that he was able to launch an attack. Had the Celtic tribes presented a united front to the enemy, Caesar might have found himself in serious difficulties.

An attack by two legions captured the *oppidum*, with many prisoners and cattle, but Cassivellaunus and his main fighting strength got away. The British confederacy still held together : at Cassivellaunus' command the Kentish forces made a bold but unsuccessful attack on Caesar's base-camp, with the objective, presumably, of destroying his ships. If this had succeeded, Caesar would have indeed been in trouble : it would have been more than a *quid pro quo* for

the loss of Wheathampstead. But it failed, and Caesar's successes were beginning to attract some British tribes to his
allegiance. Five small tribes, whose territories we do not
know, had surrendered before the fall of Wheathampstead :
more important, the powerful Trinovantes, foes to the Catuvellauni, had sought Caesar's protection and asked him to
give them a ruler. And a ruler was to hand in their prince
Mandubracius, who had been driven out by Cassivellaunus
and sought refuge with Caesar in Gaul. Here was an agent
for the advance of Roman influence in Britain as opportunity arose. Meanwhile the summer was passing : Gaul was
becoming ever more restless : a negotiated peace suited both
Caesar and Cassivellaunus. Caesar, of course, represents the
initiative as coming from the British King : the fact that
Commius was used as intermediary suggests that this was not
so. Hostages were demanded, naturally : tribute was im-
posed and the annual amounts of payment laid down. Cassivellaunus was strictly required to leave Mandubracius and
the Trinovantes alone. But Cassivellaunus retained his kingdom, and we do not know whether the tribute was ever
paid. Then Caesar led his forces back to the Channel coast.
Troops and prisoners necessitated two crossings to Gaul.
Once again storms intervened. The ships that returned
empty, together with sixty ships Labienus had constructed
as reinforcement, mostly failed to appear. Caesar had to
crowd his men together for the final crossing, shortly before
21 September. Luckily the weather was calm and none of
the transports was lost. He was not destined to see Britain
again. Vercingetorix, the Civil War, the Dictatorship, were
to fill the ten years that were left before the Ides of March.

Whether a British province had a place in that great file
of unfinished projects left by Caesar's death we cannot say –
nor, if it had, how high a priority it might have held. He had
shown that such a province might be set up, in the south-east
of Britain at least, if it were thought worth while to do so,
and provided that Gaul was pacified. Tacitus' verdict is a
fair one, that Caesar 'can be seen to have shown it [Britain]

to his successors, rather than to have made it over to them as a possession'. Yet, after all, how little Caesar had really learned about Britain can be judged from the three chapters (*De Bello Gallico*, v, 12–14) which he devoted to its geography and peoples. Short as they are, they contain a great deal of misinformation, much of which is unfortunately still reproduced in popular accounts of early British society. On the military side, sundry lessons emerge. The first is the importance of cavalry in any future Roman invading force : without them the legions would be vulnerable and seriously restricted. Caesar had shown that a balanced force of infantry and cavalry, well-handled, could sweep the Britons from the battlefield. Even more important was the need for a good land-locked harbour offering secure anchorage. Oceanus had intervened three times to protect the island and twice his intervention had been nearly fatal. For the Britons, the lessons of the two invasions need not have been wholly discouraging. The Roman army might be irresistible in the field, but guerrilla tactics could be used against it with good effect. And there was much more room for guerrilla tactics in Britain than the Romans yet knew. Above all, Caesar himself had twice invaded Britain, and twice sailed back to Gaul – the second time, never to return. When, three generations later, the Roman challenge was renewed, it is not surprising that the vastly stronger Belgic states of that time should feel that, if they could emulate their ancestors in valour, they too might win freedom for another hundred years.

## 2 Britain on the Eve of Invasion

I

In Britain political affairs at the invasion were fluid as they had not been for a generation. The death of the great King Cunobelinus in or about AD 40 removed the dominant figure whose shrewd and aggressive policy had built up a powerful Belgic Empire in south-east Britain, with its capital at Camulodunum (to use the Latin form of the name).[1] It stretched in a wide arc on either side of the Thames estuary, reaching Northamptonshire and the lands of the Coritani on the north-west, pressing hard on the frontier of the Iceni by Cambridge and Newmarket. Beyond the Thames it included northern Kent, the first lands of Belgic settlement; to the south-west it had made inroads into the kindred Belgic realm of the Atrebates – the former kingdom of Commius – in Berkshire and west Surrey. Trade and dynastic marriage had carried its influence more widely still. Among the Dobunni in the Cotswolds it seems that the state ruled from Bagendon was politically subordinate to the Belgae. The friendships and enmities aroused by this great expansion of Belgic power, though we cannot always trace them in detail, are the key to the course of the Roman invasion and to the intensive diplomacy that must have preceded it.

Economically and politically, this Belgic realm was the most advanced state in Britain. Their heavy plough and new tools made for the exploitation of richer soil than the light uplands farmed by the other British tribes. This in turn led to a denser population and a powerful army, for the Belgae had not lost the prowess of their continental ancestors, who resisted German invaders from across the Rhine and gave Caesar much hard fighting. But their main strength lay in their political organization. These Belgae had crossed from Gaul in tribal units, preserving their identity and cohesion. Indeed, the main body of the Catuvellauni appears to have migrated to Britain, leaving only a remnant in their ancestral land round Châlons on the Marne. In Britain, the royal house of the Catuvellauni had produced three great rulers – Cassivellaunus, Tasciovanus, and Cunobelinus – who between them virtually spanned the century from the invasion of Caesar to that of Claudius. These men tolerated no factious, semi-independent nobles such as those who sapped the power of other British states; if there were quarrels, they were within the royal house, and there is no sign of them before Cunobelinus' old age.

Trade further strengthened an economy founded on agriculture and war. From the Channel ports and from the Thames estuary there was easy access to the continent and the rapidly expanding market of Roman Gaul. Camulodunum became an entrepôt for the exchange of the luxury goods of the Mediterranean world – wine, pottery, metalwork, ivory and amber – with the corn, cattle, leather, gold and slaves that the Empire was willing to purchase from Britain. Strabo [2] is at pains to stress that the customs dues collected from these British exports produced more revenue than would accrue if the island were a province. The statement is, no doubt, an *apologia* for Augustus' failure to adopt a forward policy towards Britain and the extent of trade may have been exaggerated, since there is little archaeological

evidence for a large number of objects in Britain from the
Roman world before AD 43. The statement also gives what
we may take to be the official view of the force that would
be needed to hold it if it were a Roman province, 'one legion
and some cavalry' – a remarkable underestimate.

Yet archaeology warns not to exaggerate the civilization
of the Belgic realm. The excavations at Camulodunum re-
veal nothing that could be termed a city in the Greco-Roman
sense of the word. Its most striking feature, indeed, is the
complex series of earthen dykes by which it was defended, as
part of a defensive system that includes the whole of the
Colchester peninsula, some twelve square miles in extent.
The Sheepen site represents only a tiny fraction of this,
about a quarter of a square mile, and although there were
indications of the presence of a mint, and of sacred areas,[3] it
is by no means certain whether this is the Belgic settlement
which contained the residence of King Cunobelinus. There
may be other and more important sites awaiting discovery to
the east or to the south. The excavations of 1930 to 1939
were instigated as a rescue operation in advance of the construction of the Colchester by-pass. Unfortunately the later
Roman occupation of the site had seriously interfered with
the earlier structures but the dwelling-places were huts of
simple construction, round or sub-rectangular in plan. There
were no signs of any elaborate timber work and the conclusion was reached that the smaller kind of Belgic dwelling was
'a structurally primitive and squalid hovel'. The nature of
the place is, indeed, suggested by its Celtic name – Camulodunon 'the fort of Camulos' – the war-god who was the
patron divinity of the royal house of the Catuvellauni. It
cannot be denied that, so far, he had served his votaries well
during their stay in Britain.

Aggressive though it was within the island, the policy of
Cunobelinus towards Rome had always been correct and
circumspect. True, nothing is heard of the tribute which
Caesar had exacted from Cassivellaunus. But this seems to
have soon been dropped – if indeed it was ever paid. In

Cunobelinus' time it probably suited both sides to forget it. The Belgic king would have found it distasteful as a sign of submission; non-payment may also have suited Rome, for it would be a useful card to keep in reserve against some diplomatic occasion, when the demand could be presented, with arrears. When Roman soldiers were wrecked on the British coast in the great North Sea storm, they were punctiliously returned. There is no sign of meddling in Gallic politics while Cunobelinus held a firm grasp of power. But the history of Wales and Scotland provides many examples of the fatal flaw that became apparent in Celtic society when a great king approached his end, and the quarrel for succession broke out among his sons. How many sons Cunobelinus had is unknown. There cannot have been less than five – Togodumnus, Caratacus, Adminius, and the 'brothers' mentioned by Tacitus as present at the time of Caratacus' final defeat. Nothing is known of the details of the quarrel between them, only its sequel, the expulsion of Adminius and his flight to the Emperor Gaius in AD 39.[4]

The Belgic Empire was now divided between Togodumnus and Caratacus. The evidence suggests – though it does not prove – that Togodumnus ruled an eastern kingdom from Camulodunum, while Caratacus took the newly won land in the south-west, with his capital at Calleva, the old centre of the Atrebates. Both were proud Celtic princes and good generals, by the standards prevailing in Britain. Both were heirs to the imperialist tradition of their house; both shared, untempered by prudence, the anti-Roman feeling endemic for more than a century among the Belgae.

The evidence for expansion of the Belgic kingdom in the few years between Cunobelinus' death and the Claudian invasion is scanty. None the less, something can be made of the few brief references in Tacitus, Suetonius, and Dio, when they are interpreted in the light of expert analysis of the coinage of the British tribes.[5] Most of the expansion, it is clear, was the work of Caratacus. Tacitus speaks of him as 'ruling many peoples'. He is represented by two coins only (one of them doubtful), but these are in the Silchester region,[6] and it seems likely that from this base he was pushing west and south-west. A western thrust would bring him to the lands of the Dobunni, to the Cotswold area round the *oppidum* at Bagendon which bears archaeological evidence of subjection to the Catuvellauni. And, to the south-west, he would encroach further on the old Atrebatic realm that had been divided up amongst Commius' sons. There are here the coins of a certain Verica, who probably ruled at Selsey Bill, a site now under the sea, and there seems little doubt that this is the 'Bericus' mentioned by Dio[7] as taking refuge with Claudius, and providing the diplomatic excuse for Roman intervention. The stockpiling of such refugees for use if required was well-tried in Roman diplomacy. It had been used on a grand scale on the Eastern frontier with claimants and pretenders to the thrones of Parthia and Armenia. Later Agricola was to receive an Irish chieftain 'expelled by domestic strife', and keep him against an emergency.[8] Now that there were two refugees, Adminius and Bericus, in Claudius' hands, one with a claim to the old Belgic realm, the other to part of its newest conquests, it was natural enough for Togodumnus and Caratacus to demand their return, though how to interpret the armed demonstration which followed (*Britanniam tunc tumultuantem*)[9] is hard to say. Some have read into the phrase the improbable idea of an attack on the Channel coast of Gaul; this seems to postulate more naval strength than the Belgae are known to have possessed. More likely they continued to harass states friendly to Rome, whose appeals for aid would finally tip the balance in favour of invasion.

II

The other British states were far less formidable entities. Divided and broken, the old realm of Commius can only have been a secondary target for the invasion. A portion of it, that

ruled from Venta (Winchester), and including the Isle of
Wight, seems to have retained both its political freedom and
the anti-Roman feelings that Commius had brought with him
from Gaul. Much the same may have been true of the north-
western realm, in north Wiltshire and the Somerset fringe,
though here the picture is obscure. It certainly applied to
the Durotriges, a warlike though loosely-knit people whose
territory stretched from western Hampshire into East Devon.
These coastal lands also gave a home to many refugees from
Gaul, whose elaborate hill-forts were the most formidable
of their kind in Britain. Hambledon, Hod Hill, Cadbury
Castle, Maiden Castle and the rest – the Ordnance Survey
Map of Southern Britain in the Iron Age shows well over
twenty multivallate forts of more than fifteen acres in the
known territory of the tribe. These are the forts of powerful,
independent chiefs, under little if any control from a common overlord, and trying to maintain themselves in a world
of warring neighbours. In context and purpose they are like
the marcher castles of Wales. Time has denuded them now
to their earthworks, but even so they are among the most
impressive monuments in Britain as they look from height to
height across the wide green landscape of Wessex. It will remain for a later chapter to consider the military problems
that they posed.

The states so far described were, in the event, to provide
the main opposition to the Roman conquest of south-east
Britain. But the Belgic and Belgicizing peoples were ringed
by uneasy neighbours, potentially friendly to Rome, or at
least non-aligned. In Sussex and the Weald the Regni were
menaced by the expansion of the Catuvellauni into Kent
and over the Atrebates. In their large hill-forts along the
South Downs – Cissbury, Devil's Dyke, Caburn, and others –
they maintained as yet their independence. To them the
Roman invasion must have seemed a welcome prospect, and
one may suppose that they were ready to act as a bridge-
head if required. The Iceni of Norfolk and Suffolk were
in like case. They had more room for manoeuvre, and may

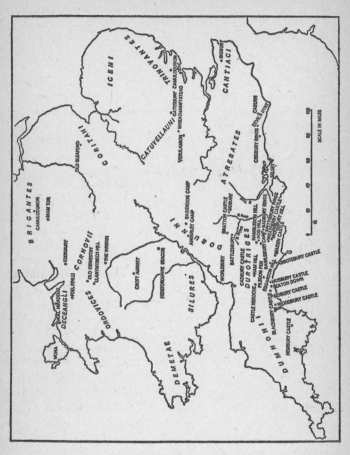

*Fig. 1: Iron Age tribes and sites to which reference is made*

well have been a more powerful tribe, but shortly before AD
43 they seem to have lost their border outposts on the Gogs
south of Cambridge,[10] and to have retreated northwards
through the Newmarket gap between the forest and the
Fens. West of the Durotriges, the Dumnonii held the whole
peninsula of Devon and Cornwall. Their hill-forts are smaller
and less elaborate than those of Wessex, some of them being
of the promontory type common in, eg, Brittany. Except for
the high land of Dartmoor and Exmoor, settlement seems to
have been extensive; it was dense in western Cornwall.
From Ictis in Mounts Bay, and probably from other ports,
there was trade with Brittany. There is no sign of a strong
central control and not much, later, of hostility to the
Roman advance. The position is more complicated with the
wealthy tribe of the Dobunni. Possessed of the good agricultural lands of the Cotswolds and of the mineral resources of
Dean (perhaps of Mendip?), minting coins and ruled by
powerful kings, theirs was a more advanced culture than
that of their kin in Dumnonia. But shortly before the Roman
invasion they became divided into a south-eastern and a
north-western realm, and the latter seems to have fallen
tributary to the rulers of Camulodunum.

Hill-forts of the Wessex type extended up the Wye and
Severn valleys as far as Old Oswestry and Llanynymech Hill.
The hills are higher and bolder on this mountainous fringe of
Wales, and there is a dramatic quality to such sites as Herefordshire Beacon, Malvern, and Croft Ambrey near Ludlow.
Tribal boundaries are uncertain, but the heartlands of the
Cornovii were in Shropshire and Cheshire, and their centre
may well have been the Wrekin.[11] Settlement must have
been thin on the high Midland plateau, but crop marks of
farmsteads are dense along the river terraces with their light
subsoils. Eastwards again lay a belt of lias and oolite more
suitable for agriculture. Here lay the lands of the Coritani,
stretching from the Warwickshire Avon to the Lincoln Wolds
and perhaps the Humber. Their position exposed them to
Belgic pressure from the south-east, and archaeological evi-

dence suggests that the Belgic dynasty ruled from a site near
Sleaford on the eve of the invasion. Beyond Humber and
Mersey the Brigantes, a confederacy of warlike peoples, held
the Pennine and Cumbrian moors and mountains under the
uneasy rule of a monarchy. In what is now the East Riding
of Yorkshire the Parisii seem to have maintained intact the
tribal identity they had brought to Britain from their Gallic
homeland between the Seine and the Marne. What is now
Wales was divided between four main tribes, whose territories correspond, roughly, to the four ancient Welsh dio-
ceses. The Demetae of the south-west are the least-known,
though in Dyfed they have left their tribal name on the land.
But the Silures of the south-east were to play a great part in
resisting the Roman conquest. Tacitus notes the physical
characteristics that marked them off from the other peoples
of Britain, and speculates about a possible Iberian origin.[12]
The Plain of Gwent gave them a good tract of agricultural
land, and the Black Mountains and Brecon Beacons a natural
fortress. Mona (Anglesey) and the mountains of Eryri played
the same role for the Ordovices, whose fighting spirit was en-
hanced by the presence in Mona of the headquarters of the
Druids. In Britain as in Gaul, this priesthood fostered pan-
Celtic and anti-Roman feeling. Between Conway and Dee
were the Deceangli : their hill-forts, of the Wessex type,
stretch above the Clwydian range. The name survives in
Deganwy (?) and the medieval Tegeingl.

### III

This survey has touched on all the British states involved in
any way in the Claudian conquest. It is to be noted that the
invasion was preceded by an intensive phase of diplomacy,
an arm which Rome exploited against the barbarian peoples
no less effectively than war. On the Rhine and Danube frontiers in particular, dealing with military problems far more
intractable than those of Britain, the cool head and long experience of Tiberius had shown what could be done by pro-

voking and sustaining the enmities endemic among the tribes. Tacitus shows this policy in action at a dramatic moment – in AD 16 immediately after Germanicus had won his great victory at the Battle of Idistaviso. The Roman commander believed that the enemy were flagging : 'one more summer in the field, and the German war could be wound up'. But he kept getting letters from Tiberius advising him to return and celebrate the Triumph already voted.

We have had enough [said the Emperor] of successes and disasters. You have won great victories, but you must also remember what the winds and waves have done – through no fault of the commander – to cause grievous and heavy loss. I was sent into Germany by Augustus nine times, and I achieved more by diplomacy than by war. That was how the Sugambri surrendered, how the Suebi and King Maroboduus were induced to keep the peace. As for the Cherusci and the other bellicose tribes, the vengeance of Rome has been duly provided for. Now we can leave them to quarrel among themselves.

No Roman could speak out of a fuller knowledge of the peoples of northern Europe. He had seen their inveterate tendency to quarrel among themselves allow Rome to pass safely through the moment of supreme peril – when after the disaster to Varus in AD 9 the victorious Arminius had besought the Marcomanni to join him in a great offensive against Roman power. The barbarians could be relied upon to quarrel after a war, they could be softened up by diplomacy before it began.

So now, in Britain, offers of client kingship would have kept some British rulers out of the struggle. Strabo [13] tells us that British kings visited Augustus in Rome and made offerings in the Capitol which, as has been pointed out,[14] could only signify the ratification of treaties. Thus at least two of the British tribes had already entered into a relationship with

Rome which may have lasted into the time of Claudius, and may have been recognized after AD 43 by the creation of client kingships for the Iceni and for Cogidubnus. The latter emerges as one of the leading Britons in the Roman province, but his place in the invasion and conquest must be considered later.

If the main terms were known in advance it explains why the Senate was prepared to allow Claudius *carte blanche* in ratifying the settlement of British affairs.[15] But the biggest piece on the board eluded the skill of the Roman negotiators. This was, of course, to force a breach between Togodumnus and Caratacus. A passage in Tacitus[16] suggests that it was tried, for in his speech before Claudius Caratacus refers to a period of success and prosperity, in which prudence on his part could have led to a treaty of friendship with Rome. The best context for such a proposition would be that of negotiations immediately before the invasion. But loyalty held between the brothers, and they resolved to direct the united forces of their kingdoms against the Romans.

We are nowhere told how many men they were able to put into the field, though some sort of estimate may be made. In the few weeks of the campaign, their forces fought two holding operations, then a two-day battle on the Medway against the full strength of the invading army, next a cavalry action after the Thames crossing, and perhaps (though this is doubtful) a further action to dispute the advance to Camulodunum. There still remained enough fighting men for an effective force to follow Caratacus to Wales. The Medway battle is the key. To hold up a Roman army of some 40,000 would surely call for a British force substantially larger, of at least 60,000 men. It is not extravagant to suppose that the Belgic princes could mobilize 80,000 men or more. This in turn would suggest a population of at least 400,000 from which they could be drawn, according to the formula which no less an authority than Caesar used to estimate Gallic population and resources.[17] Some comparisons may be helpful. The Helvetii who invaded Gaul in 58 BC reckoned their

total number, with their allies, at 368,000, of whom 90,000
were fighting men. These were defeated by Caesar near
Bibracte with an army of six legions and auxiliaries. The
great host mustered against him by the Belgae in 57 BC was
said by Gallic observers to number almost 300,000 – a figure
which has rightly provoked scepticism. With 40,000 men,
and the advantage of carefully chosen ground, Caesar was
able to defeat them and cause them to disperse. At Neuf-
Mesnil the Nervii, most warlike of the Belgic peoples, gave
Caesar's six legions a desperate fight with an army of 60,000
men. Diodorus Siculus, following Posidonius, says that the
larger Gallic states could field an army of about 200,000
men; the smaller, about 50,000.[18] Like all ancient estimates
of population, these figures can only be accepted with
caution. But they do give an order of magnitude, if not an
actual figure, and they do not suggest that the resources of
Cunobelinus' realm were equal to those of the greater Gallic
states of Caesar's day.

Since the Belgic decision to oppose Rome led to military
disaster and the end of their kingdoms' independence, it is
tempting to ask why it ever seemed valid. Here again we may
look to Tacitus. To the British observer, Rome's record in
north-western Europe might not seem impressive – at least,
not since the victories of Julius Caesar. The disaster inflicted
on Varus by Arminius in AD 9 had not really been erased by
the prestige victories won by Germanicus. Augustus' advice
to maintain the frontiers of the Empire as he had left them
had been a realistic appraisal, loyally accepted by Tiberius.
Gaius' attempt to breach it had been a fiasco. And who was
Claudius, if not the most unmilitary of emperors? Again, the
Britons were sustained by their own interpretation of the
invasions of Julius Caesar. Tacitus makes Caratacus, and
later Boudicca, invoke the memory of Caesar's defeat and
withdrawal from the island.[19] The delay before the troops
of Claudius could be got to embark must have encouraged
the belief that invasion was not seriously intended; the
appeal to the deeds of their ancestors, that it could be de-

feated. A credible picture could be built up, by men not naturally gifted at reckoning the odds. Tacitus, Caesar, and Livy all emphasize the recklessness of the Celts in pitting themselves against danger, and their irresolution once it had come. One thinks of Bituitus, the great king of the Arverni, watching with confidence the armies of Domitius Ahenobarbus and Fabius Maximus moving to battle positions. 'They are too few to feed my hounds!' was his contemptuous remark.[20] They were enough to win the battle that secured for Rome a permanent hold on Southern Gaul. The *audacia* of Caratacus and Togodumnus was of a different order, but proceeded from the same cause: the determination of brave men to defend their freedom without counting too closely the cost.

No classical writer discusses at any length the Roman motives for the invasion. The fact is significant: it was not thought to require elaborate justification. This has not deterred modern scholars from propounding numerous and conflicting theories,[21] the need to exploit British minerals, to complete the Romanization of Gaul, to suppress Druidism, to break up the dangerous concentration of military strength along the Rhine, to win personal glory for Claudius, and so on. Armed with the knowledge of hindsight, and in the light of the difficulties Rome encountered in the highland zone of Britain and of her ultimate failure in Scotland, they have been inclined to doubt the wisdom of the whole British venture. To argue thus is to ignore the situation of AD 43 and the objectives at which the invasion itself was aimed. Julius Caesar's British expeditions had bequeathed to his successors an unfinished task. He had set up a simulacrum of Roman authority in south-east Britain that had failed to produce results. Augustus had shown a wish to come to grips with the problem, but had been distracted. Tiberius had followed his advice not to advance the Imperial frontiers. The abortive plans of Gaius had led to a dangerous loss of prestige. Now, with the death of Cunobelinus and the quarrels among his sons, the time was ripe to secure a Roman hold on the most civilized and the most dangerous part of the island by reducing the Belgic Empire to a Roman Province. Seen in this light, the Claudian invasion appears to have aimed at a limited objective and promised a valuable return.

## 3 The Invasion and the Defeat of the Belgic Kingdom

I

Any account of the invasion must begin with a recognition of the sketchy nature of the historical sources. The episode will have been treated at length by Tacitus in the *Annals*, but the books dealing with the years AD 37–47 are missing. The loss is irreparable. The only continuous narrative we have is that of Dio Cassius – a very inferior substitute.[1] Dio wrote in the early third century – nearly two hundred years after the invasion – and we do not know and cannot evaluate the sources he used. Two inscriptions, one from the Arch of Claudius in Rome, the other from the contemporary arch at Cyzicus, give a brief but invaluable glimpse of the official line.[2] Two paragraphs of Suetonius' *Lives* (*Claudius* and *Vespasian*) offer marginal and anecdotal information.[3] Archaeological evidence amplifies some points, but to a less extent than could be wished. Such are the narrow limits within which we must work.

Embarkation accomplished, the Roman command could put into operation their plans for the next phase. Two hazards confront the invader of Britain – the fight in the Channel and the opposed landing. It seems to us natural that the islanders should muster whatever fleet they maintain and engage the invader at sea. When that fleet disposes of formidable striking power, the invader may never dare to leave the coasts of the continent. This is what pinned down Napoleon's troops at Boulogne. The invasion-barges and warships that Hitler had assembled seemed a menace through the long and terrible weeks of the late summer of 1940, but it was a menace that never materialized. The fate of the Spanish Armada is a signal example of what may be in store for the invader : *afflavit Deus et dissipati sunt*. But William of Normandy crossed unopposed, and the prospect of a naval engagement was not one of the anxieties of Aulus Plautius. For the last 'native' sea-power in these waters had been that of the Veneti, defeated by Caesar. No other was to appear until the ships of the Saxons challenged the *classis Britannica* under Carausius in the late third century, or those of King Niall of the Nine Hostages cruised in the Irish Sea and the English Channel in the fourth. Had Cunobelinus anticipated Alfred in raising a fleet . . . but such a venture was far beyond the horizon of any of the British states.

The opposed landing was another matter. No commander, ancient or modern, has relished the idea of landing his forces in the teeth of enemy opposition. Notoriously, Caesar's first expedition to Britain (55 BC) had run into serious difficulties on this very point. The famous standard bearer of the Xth Legion, leaping into the sea and calling on his men to follow, was an episode more edifying to read about than to see repeated.[4] How to avoid an engagement on these terms must have been a major problem for the staff tacticians. Dio's statement that the Roman forces sailed in three divisions is a pointer to their solution. This was done, he says, 'to avoid the hindrance in landing that might delay a single force'. Would this hindrance come from the beach-head selected, inadequate for so large a force? Or from the enemy? The latter seems more likely. In their appreciation of the problem, the Roman staff must have assumed that a strong British force would be maintained along the coast. A general alarm once given, the Britons would prepare to defend the beaches. But if a decoy force could be used to deceive the Britons as to Roman intentions, an unopposed landing might be possible at the point selected for the main attack. The care with which this selection was made does credit to the Roman staff-work, for they discovered by far the best possible place. The key to it is the Wantsum Channel, then a broad navigable channel separating Thanet from the mainland. At its southern entrance and off the western shore lay a sizeable island, site of the later Rutupiae, and of a Saxon Shore fort. Even in the drained landscape of today it is conspicuous across the flats from Sandwich, rising as it does fifty-eight feet above sea-level. In Roman times a navigable channel came up to its eastern side, and it offered an area of dry ground for the safe unloading of men and stores. Once this was secured, other factors would come into play. The Wantsum Channel itself was virtually a landlocked roadstead, and a long sandspit running out from the southern point of Thanet would further protect the Richborough anchorage. Direct access to the Thames – at least at high tide – would make it unnecessary for ships to round the North Foreland. A British attack on the position would have to cross the channel to the west of the island in the face of Roman sea-power. On the mainland, a ridge of high ground would offer good going for a Roman thrust against the Canterbury area, where was in all likelihood the nearest main centre of British power. And finally, if the worst should happen, it would be possible for Aulus Plautius to draw off his troops and transports without undue loss. The search for a good beach-head has occupied many commanders at many periods of history, on both sides of the Channel. Seldom can a position have offered so many advantages to the invading forces as the island of Rutupiae.

Two other things emerge in Dio's account of the crossing. Contrary winds drove back the Roman Fleet, and the crossing was made at night as those of Caesar had been. 'They became disheartened at being driven back . . . but recovered their spirits when they saw a flash of light rise in the east and shoot across to the west – the direction of their course.' It is impossible to determine whether this night crossing was accidental – the result of headwinds – or deliberately planned. If the latter, the invasion scheme must have provided for the main force to embark in the late afternoon, cross the Channel under cover of darkness, and land in the early dawn.

Something of the anxieties of that night filter through into Dio's narrative. An invading army, sailing towards an enemy shore, is in a situation which concentrates the mind wonderfully – as Dr Johnson remarked of the man about to be hanged. Perhaps some of the officers, when they saw the bright flash, recalled that other meteor which had induced Anchises to leave Troy, launching Aeneas and his followers into their high destiny. The nervous tension of the troops was no doubt heightened by this portent, and they will have needed a steadying remark such as that produced by the Greek general Epaminondas on a similar occasion, and recorded by Frontinus : 'The heavenly powers have sent us this light.' Less famous and less striking than the appearance of Halley's comet which heralded the triumph of William of Normandy in 1066, the meteor of that late summer night of AD 43 none the less urged forward the invaders of Britain. Ahead of the fleet that evening of late summer lay the four hundred years of Roman Britain, the roads and the cities and the villas, the flames of Boudicca's rebellion, and the bitter years of fighting in the north. But soldiers do not have these long thoughts. Each man must have speculated on the unknown coastline that lay ahead, the enemy assault, and his own prospects in the fight on the beach.

II

The operation so far described called for two forces – main and decoy. The decoy force perhaps made a landfall by the cliffs of Dover and turned west to draw the Britons away from the main landing. What of the third force mentioned by Dio? For this one needs to consider the possibility of the Romans making a link with a force of British allies. As shown above, Roman diplomacy had skilfully maintained a foothold in Britain, and it could be established that there was a sound political justification for the invasion, since the Romans were coming to the aid of an ally. It is also certain that the principal ally was the tribe of the Atrebates, whose neighbours the Regni held one of the best anchorages along the whole south-east coast, in Chichester harbour. Reviewing the events from the distance of many centuries, it would seem obvious strategy for the army to make this their main base of operation. But the Roman dislike of the sea and the considerable extra distance along the coast undoubtedly led to the use of the shorter crossing to Rutupiae and the Kentish harbours for the main force.

One of the key figures in this phase must have been the chieftain Cogidubnus, who eventually emerges as *rex et legatus Augusti in Britannia*. These titles appear on an inscription found in Chichester in 1723, now built into the wall of the Town Hall (see Appendix II, p. 163). It records the building of a temple to Neptune and Minerva by the guild of smiths and metalworkers. The selection of deities suggests that the guild was closely connected with shipping; they may have been shipwrights or chandlers. The erection of such a building could hardly have taken place soon after the invasion as time must be allowed for the founding of the town and the development of its industries to the point when there was a guild wealthy enough to finance such an enterprise. Cogidubnus lived long enough for Tacitus to recall that he had been faithful to Rome 'till our own day', implying that the British king was still alive in the seventies.[5] The balance of probability is that this inscription must be dated to this late period and therefore it offers no proof that Cogidubnus received his title of *legatus Augusti in Britannia* from Claudius. Indeed it is hardly likely that Claudius would have done more than make him a Roman citizen and client king. The names Tiberius Claudius taken by Cogidubnus showed that he owed this honour at least to Claudius, but the second title, that of Imperial Legate, is a different matter.[6] The words of Tacitus when he refers to Cogidubnus suggest that that monarch had occasion to demonstrate his loyalty at a later date, and it is not difficult to suggest an occasion. As will be seen below, the general responsible for the conquest of the south-west was Vespasian, and during his arduous campaign he would have needed bases in friendly hands. There is archaeological evidence that one of these was at Fishbourne (see p. 82) not far from the new capital of Cogidubnus (Noviomagus, at Chichester). Vespasian would certainly have had a very close and amicable relationship with the British king, and the future Emperor was not a man to forget his old cronies. There was a time in the civil war of AD 68–9 when there was divided loyalty among the legions of Britain. As the star of Vespasian gained its ascendant the presence in Britain of an old friend and loyal supporter may have been critical in preventing the legions from joining the opposing side. Vitellius could muster only token forces from Britain and the Governor, Vettius Bolanus, prevaricated when pressed for more. If Cogidubnus had been active on behalf of Vespasian, here was a time when it could have been rewarded. Election to the Roman Senate at this time would have caused no eyebrows to be raised and the extraordinary title (which is difficult to explain in any other context) could be considered merely as a high honour to the King, now an old man. The title would have given equality with the Governor, in itself an awkward anomaly in any other circumstances.[7]

Another version of the events of this period has been presented.[8] This ingenious hypothesis introduces another character into the situation – Cn Sentius Saturninus, who had been consul in 41 and was a man of some importance, although junior to the new Governor, Aulus Plautius. He escapes mention in Dio but appears linked with Plautius in the brief account of the invasion given by the fourth-

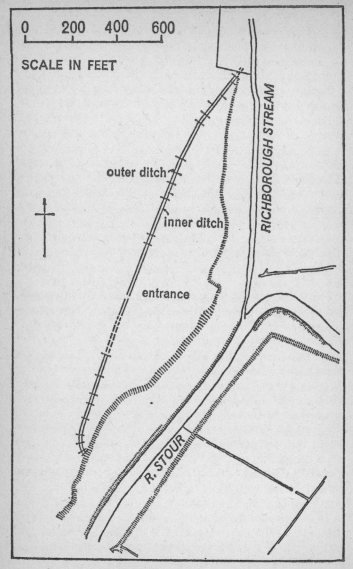

0  200  400  600

SCALE IN FEET

outer ditch

inner ditch

entrance

RICHBOROUGH STREAM

R. STOUR

*Fig. 2: The Claudian camp at Richborough*

century historian Eutropius.[9] It is suggested that Sentius was given a diplomatic appointment and sent to Britain with Cogidubnus to meet the British kings and come to terms with them. The Briton would have been the negotiator fulfilling the role Commius did for Caesar in Britain in 55 BC. Sentius Saturninus, with the powers of an Imperial Legate, could have signed treaties and given undertakings in an attempt to win over the wavering loyalties of some of the kings of Britain. The task completed, Cogidubnus – according to this theory – took over the titles held by Sentius Saturninus. It is a most attractive idea, but this is too weighty a superstructure to be built on the introduction of his name by Eutropius. It is known that a number of important senators accompanied Claudius to Britain as his *comites* or advisory council. Sentius Saturninus was a man of uncertain loyalty [10] and would have been too dangerous to leave behind in Rome. Thus a much more rational and simple explanation can be found.

There seems little doubt that Cogidubnus was of material assistance in the initial stages of the conquest; none that he was rewarded with citizenship and a kingdom. He may have acted as a negotiator on behalf of Plautius or he may have had command of a small force which landed at Fishbourne and operated on the long exposed flank of the Britons. He may even have secured the bridge over the Thames. Perhaps we shall never know the answer. But finds at Chichester attest the presence of legionaries at this period – whether they came at this stage of the advance or when the place was a base for operations under Vespasian in the same year it is quite impossible to decide. It would indeed be a most remarkable discovery that could distinguish between sites and objects so close together in time.

It is time to return to Richborough, which we have postulated as a key point for the invasion. Excavations have shown that, apart from traces of the Early Iron Age, the earliest occupation of the site was associated with Claudian coins, pottery and military equipment.[11] The structural remains of this phase consist of two parallel V-shaped ditches of typical military profile with an entrance and causeway. These ditches were traced for a total length of 705 yards and there was definite evidence of a corner at the southern limit, but only a slight turn at the north end. The east side of the site is bounded by the River Stour and the Richborough stream, which flows through what is now a low-lying marshy area. Considerable physical changes have taken place on the sea-ward side, with the silting of the Wantsum Channel and the total disappearance of the Roman harbour. It is nevertheless doubtful if much land has been lost by encroachment or erosion; though the walls of the Saxon Shore fort on its east side have been undermined and fallen outwards, they may well have been built at the edge of the sea. In effect then, the area contained by the Claudian ditches was much the same as it is today – about ten acres. When the Roman Army camped, their leather tents were set out in orderly array at an approximate concentration of 250 men per acre. This landing base would therefore have held about 2,500 men, no more than a task force sent over to secure a bridge-head.

Bushe-Fox concludes from his examination of the ditches that they were in being for only a short time and states that 'the earthwork was without doubt formed as a temporary defence to cover the disembarkation of the troops at the time of the invasion and to serve as a protection for the ships drawn up on to the shore during the initial stages of the campaign in AD 43. There is no evidence of a heavy occupation at this period, and only a small detachment may have been in garrison there: it may even have been left derelict for several years.' If Richborough had been the main base surely more forces would have arrived and been accommodated. There is certainly enough room on the plateau to the west; if the camp of ten acres was an initial landing base for the task force, the ditches would have been quickly filled in and a much larger area taken over for 30–40,000 men. This would have required a camp of 120–160 acres. Very little

excavation has been carried out beyond the area of the
Saxon Shore fort[12] and it is possible that the defences of
such a large camp may yet be found.

As soon as the army was established in Britain, the value
of the land-locked harbour at Richborough became apparent. The next stage was the erection of a large store-base.
Some of its timber buildings can be identified as granaries
since the floors are built on a series of uprights, well above
the ground level, with an air space between, thus avoiding
the effect of damp and entry by small animals.[13] These buildings remained in position until early Flavian times, but they
probably went out of use at a much earlier date, once supplies could have been taken to more convenient points nearer
the military bases.

III

Wherever the landing – or landings – took place, the important fact is that they were unopposed. Not only that, but
Plautius found no large British force in the vicinity. Dio tells
us that the Britons were tired of waiting and had gone home.
The delay caused by the refusal to embark had led to the dis-
persal of the British levies. The mutiny had been of benefit,
after all. It would have been difficult for the Belgic chiefs to
hold their men together for any length of time. There was no
standing professional army; the only troops, apart from the
aristocratic warriors and their personal followers, were the
British farmers, taken from their unremitting tasks to wait
for an army which never came. As the days and weeks went
by and rumours of mutiny in the Roman Army were brought
in, it is hardly surprising that the Belgic war-lords decided
that there had been another fiasco, and yielded to the pressure of levies anxious to return to their farms and families.

This explains why Plautius 'had some difficulty in finding
the Britons'. R. G. Collingwood conjured up a vivid picture
of the harassed general marching and counter-marching up
and down Kent with one eye on Caesar's commentaries and

the other on the depopulated Kentish landscape.[14] This is over-imaginative. Plautius may have been surprised at the absence of Britons but he set about the very necessary task of establishing his base with its supplies while light units gently probed into Kent. Unlike Caesar he did not take advantage of the situation and rush boldly forward to seize points of strategic importance. It is probable that the tribes of east Kent rapidly came to terms with the Romans as soon as their strength and purpose were revealed.

Meanwhile the two leaders of the Belgae had not been idle. As soon as news reached them of the landing they decided on a strategy of reassembling their main armies at the Medway crossing, where the issue was to be decided. Doubtless with a view to delaying the Roman advance, at least two skirmishes were fought by the two brothers on separate occasions or places. Plautius, says Dio, first defeated Caratacus, then Togodumnus. Caratacus, if he had been ruling the south-western kingdom, would naturally make the first contact with the Romans. The fact that they were operating independently at this stage need not have been bad tactics if it was to shield the main build-up of strength behind them and to test the Roman strength.

Before the main battle a curious event is inserted – the capitulation of the 'Bodunni'. This episode has been subject to close study by Professor C. F. C. Hawkes and in a most ingenious and convincing line of argument he suggests that this was a levy of a section of the Dobunni from Gloucestershire.[15] The coin evidence now suggests that this tribe was divided into two parts. The northernmost had its headquarters at Bagendon near Cirencester, and the finds there indicate either a very strong trading and cultural relationship with the Catuvellauni, or, what seems more likely, their actual conquest. The southern part of the tribe occupying south Gloucestershire and north Somerset did not share the same degree of Belgic influence, and, as Professor Hawkes has argued, these peoples were probably descendants of a westward extension of the Atrebates. Had the northern part of the Dobunni been assimilated by Belgic culture, it is not likely that they would have been so eager to capitulate to Plautius; that they did so is suggestive of enslavement and enforced levies raised against Rome. Earlier historians attempted to involve Plautius in an invasion of the southwest, since Dio appears to state that a garrison was planted in 'their', ie Dobunnic territory. Professor Hawkes argues that the Greek word *entautha* used by Dio need not mean this, but simply 'thereupon'. In other words, Plautius received this surrender and thereupon, leaving a garrison behind – the normal method of consolidating gains – continued his advance.

Next he came to a river. 'The barbarians thought that the Romans would not be able to cross it without a bridge and consequently bivouacked in a rather careless fashion on the opposite bank.' The only river which would fit these conditions in Kent is the Medway. The main route followed by the Roman Army was probably the ancient prehistoric trackway along the North Downs which was later to become famous as the Pilgrims' Way along which Chaucer's company rode to the shrine of Thomas à Becket at Canterbury. There are several crossing points of the river between Aylesford and Rochester, but most of them would have been suitable only for small parties with pack animals. The river below Aylesford pursues a winding course through marshy and wooded ground where access to its banks would have been difficult. The obvious crossing point for a large army would have been immediately above Rochester, where there is firm ground on both sides down to the river edge and excellent visibility along the river from the heights on the east bank. This is the point chosen by the engineers who have designed the course of the Medway motorway, whose bridge almost straddles the ancient crossing. Here of course the river is tidal, and the ford may only have been usable at low tide; this may account for the time it took the Romans to secure their bridge-head. It should be added that the hill now occupied by Borstal would provide the Roman commander with an admirable grandstand view of the battle-field. A similar but more distant position is available for the British command on the west bank (8).

The Roman army may have had qualms about an opposed landing from the sea, but for river-crossings they were well trained and equipped. The section in Frontinus' *Stratagems* devoted to river-crossings concentrates on the element of surprise and outflanking manoeuvres. Moreover, the Romans had specialist troops for just such an operation. These were the Frisian and Batavian cavalry regiments whose experience in the Low Countries had accustomed them to crossing such barriers and fighting in waterlogged terrain. We meet them in the *Annals* of Tacitus doing good service in Germanicus' northern campaigns, and they were to do even better in Britain in such operations as the crossing of the Menai Straits.[16] Dio's account of the Medway operation is very sketchy :

He (Plautius) sent across Gallic troops who were trained to swim with full equipment across the swiftest of rivers. Surprise was achieved . . . by this attack : they did not shoot at the men themselves : instead, wounding the horses that drew their chariots, they made it impossible even for the charioteers to get away in the subsequent confusion. At this point Plautius sent across Flavius Vespasianus (the future Emperor), and his elder brother Sabinus, who was acting as his lieutenant.[17] This force also succeeded in crossing the river, and killing many of the barbarians, who were not expecting them. The rest of the British forces however did not retreat, but on the next day joined issue with them again. There was an indecisive struggle, but at last Gnaeus Hosidius Geta (after being almost taken prisoner) managed to defeat them. For this achievement he was later awarded the *ornamenta triumphalia*, though he had never been consul. Then the Britons retired. . .

Embodied in this unsatisfactory account are some of the elements of a great battle, lasting two days, which settled the fate of Britain for the next four centuries.

The best attempt to make sense of it is that of Mr A. R. Burn,[18] and we accept and follow his main points, though suggesting a different site for the battle. Dio's account appears to describe two separate crossings of the river. In the first the Gallic *auxilia* make a diversion by swimming over and attacking the British horses. The presence of chariots at this point suggests that the bank was held by tribal chieftains. The main purpose of this attack seems to have been to distract the attention of the Britons from the second crossing, which was made by the legionaries. The comment of Dio that they were not expected implies that this later crossing was made at another point, and that the army had carried out an outflanking operation, probably upstream, while the Britons were dealing with what they may have thought the main attack.

The legion chosen for this was the IInd *Augusta* under its commander Vespasian. Having secured a foothold on the opposite bank, his next step was probably to bring up a pontoon bridge or ferry boats to build up strength. The need for equipment to ford a river and establish rapid access to the bridge-head would have been considered in the initial planning of the campaign, though the Thames may then have been in mind. The heavy train brought up in the rear of the advancing army would have included many kinds of equipment, mainly for siege work.

These operations occupied the first day. The Britons soon realized that the main threat came from the new bridge-head and that, unless they were able to wipe it out rapidly and completely, its strength would grow until they would have to deal with the main force of the army on the west bank of the river. Meanwhile, perhaps through the night, fresh legionaries had been poured into the bridge-head. There was now more than one legion, and a task force commander, Hosidius Geta, presumably the senior legionary *legatus*,[19] took over. Now came the critical stage. In the daylight hours of the second day the Britons gathered their full strength and flung themselves into the assault. They managed to drive a deep wedge into the Roman ranks and almost succeeded in splitting their opponents. Geta was nearly captured, and he would have been stationed in a central or even rearward position at Staff HQ. But as more and fresh troops were poured across the Medway into the bridge-head the balance of strength changed. The Britons had spent themselves, and the Roman Army was ready to break out of its confined space into open order. The Britons retired, the Roman Army was left in full possession. The Battle of Britain of AD 43 was over. Although it was not fully appreciated at the time, the fate of Britain had been sealed.

It is difficult to believe that such a violent clash would not have left some permanent mark on the landscape. The Roman Army must have built temporary camps for their forces of the usual geometric pattern. So far nothing has been observed either from the air or on the ground resembling these features. Of the great battle there is only one archaeological trace, and that found as recently as 1958. This consists of a hoard of thirty-four gold coins found in the village of Bredgar[20] on the North Downs. The latest of these coins are four of Claudius struck during AD 41 and 42. This hoard, almost four years' pay for a private, may be the savings of an officer, buried for safety before the engagement and never reclaimed. The find spot, nine miles from Aylesford, lies on the Downs just before the descent towards the Medway; it may have been the site of one of the camps where the assault troops rested before the battle. What has been identified as a 'fortlet' below the later Saxon Shore fort at Reculver[21] may belong to the period of the initial advance since it would have been necessary to have had holding detachments in the rear, especially to watch the Estuary.

The course of the river battle, thus reconstructed from the scrappy notes of Dio, has a very modern ring. There is a swift crossing at an unexpected point to secure a foothold, however precarious, until armour can be pushed across. If the bridge-head can be pinched out at this stage before the real fighting strength is there, the venture fails. But Roman discipline and toughness just managed to hold the bridge-head until the tables could be turned. It was no easy victory, but a long and bitter struggle against an heroic and determined foe, ably led. But the Romans were unable to follow up rapidly as their cavalry *auxilia* were on the other bank. By the time they were brought across and set off in pursuit the Britons had executed a speedy withdrawal.

Dio continues :

Thence the Britons fell back to the River Thames at a point near where it enters the sea and forms a large pool at high tide. Knowing the firm ground and the fords with much precision, they crossed the river without difficulty; but the Romans were not so successful. However, the Celts swam across again and some others got over by a bridge a little way upstream, after which they assailed the barbarians from several sides at once and cut down many of them. In pursuing the remainder incautiously, they got into swamps from which it was difficult to make their way out and so lost a number of men.

The situation seems clear enough. The British command managed to break off the engagement, withdraw the bulk of their men, and make an escape across the Thames into the Essex marshes. There are several low-lying places like the Erith Marshes along the Thames which might in those days have been flooded at high tide. Woe betide anyone venturing into these areas without any knowledge of the firm paths! The main problem in Dio's account is the mention of a bridge further upstream, which appears to have been left intact and unguarded. It would seem strange tactics for such a resourceful leader as Caratacus to have left the main route to Camulodunum so unguarded. Did he give in so easily or were there other factors not mentioned? There seems no doubt that the most difficult task facing the Roman Army was that of crossing the Thames, a very different proposition from the Medway. Plautius would have known some of the difficulties from a study of Caesar : how the river was only just fordable in one place and how the Britons had, in 54 BC, protected the opposite bank by a fence of sharp stakes which continued below water level. Plautius may have known about the bridge from the traders who had probably already established a depôt nearby. Had the Romans managed to capture the bridge by surprise tactics? This brings us back to the possibility of a landing at Chichester. It would not have been impossible for the Atrebates, with Roman cavalry support, to make their way by forest paths across the heavy Wealden clays, and swoop suddenly down on the small British force detailed to hold the bridge. Did the British forces turn to cross the Thames into Essex because the pursuit was too hot, or had they heard that the bridge had fallen?

The heavy Medway defeat, followed so quickly by the loss of the bridge, showed all too clearly the strength and organization of the Roman Army and must have thrown out all the plans of Caratacus. By now there would be news of the other British tribes. Some were already won over : now, as the conquerors showed their teeth, more would flock to the Roman side. His resources were now more slender, though his tribesmen and bodyguards would remain faithful. Where could he hope to hold the Romans, already probing into Essex? There was no line of natural defence between the Thames and the Belgic capital at Camulodunum. Should he die trapped behind the massive earthworks of the Colne peninsula? As he brooded over this problem more unpleasant news reached him. His brother Togodumnus had perished, presumably in some skirmish north of the Thames, or by treachery. The two brothers may not have been very close, but they were united in their hatred of Rome, and above all it was Togodumnus who could command the allegiance of the main part of the Belgic Kingdom. Perhaps some of the

Belgic nobles began to waver, especially those of Verula-mium.

Whatever dark thoughts Caratacus may have harboured, he must have realized that there was no hope of holding up the Roman advance towards the Belgic capital, and that once there the end would come swiftly. He was not alone in these forebodings. One of the great powers in Britain was the Druids. So much imaginative nonsense has been written about these priests and their cult that they are often dismissed by serious historians as unworthy of discussion. Their real power lay not so much in their secret rites, as in their control over the Celtic tribal aristocracy. It was the Druids who were responsible for the education of the children of the kings and notables. Their high priests were drawn from these ranks, and so accepted by the kings as advisers in matters political as well as religious. Nor were the Druids the special preserve of a particular tribe. They claimed universal support from all the Celtic peoples, not only in Britain but in Gaul as well. They were thus a strong unifying force in the Celtic world, as Caesar had found in Gaul. All their resources were now bent on holding back the influence of Rome. Druidism because of its strong anti-Roman political feeling could not survive in a Roman province. The Roman government, accepting any form of religion which did not meddle in politics, was prepared to stamp out Druidism with complete ruthlessness. Another example of this attitude is seen in the Jewish Wars later in the first century. Judaism had pitted itself against Rome, and the headquarters of the national religion, the Great Temple in Jerusalem, was destroyed with a savage thoroughness. The Druids in Britain would never compromise, and to them the *pax Romana* was anathema. To survive at all resistance must be continued, and Caratacus was their best instrument. They clearly saw the only hope of success in a withdrawal as far west as the Welsh mountains. Here was terrain which could be defended, and in it lived a tough hill-folk with courage and tenacity far exceeding that of the farmers of Essex. Caratacus, no doubt, saw this, but he had no standing in Wales. Now the headquarters of the Druids were in Mona (Anglesey), and the recent and famous find of treasure, the remains of a ritual deposit, from Llyn Cerrig Bach [22] attest their influence over the tribes of Britain. Theirs would have been the influence which commended Caratacus to the tribes of Wales, and secured his election as war-leader.

But, if Caratacus went to Wales, other leaders maintained a spirit of defiance among the Belgae. Dio relates :

> Shortly afterwards Togodumnus perished, but the Britons, so far from yielding, united all the more firmly to avenge his death. Because of this fact and because of the difficulties he had encountered at the Thames, Plautius became afraid, and instead of advancing any further, proceeded to guard what he had already won, and sent for Claudius. For he had been instructed to do this in case he met with any particularly stubborn resistance and, in fact, extensive equipment including elephants had already been got together for the expedition.

This curious and paradoxical passage seems to contain garbled pieces of an official report, that of the commander to his emperor. Plautius found himself in a dilemma. He, had, thanks to the prowess of his army and good staff-work, subdued the main opposition in the lowlands of Britain. The way to the capital, Camulodunum, was open, and he must have soon realized that any further resistance once the Thames was crossed could hardly be serious. If he was not careful Plautius might find himself actually on the point of entering Camulodunum. This would have exceeded his instructions, as Dio makes apparent. Only the Imperator himself should lead his victorious troops into the enemy capital. A carefully worded dispatch must therefore be sent to Claudius, outlining all the difficulties to be overcome, and how the legate now found himself unable to proceed further without the leadership of the emperor in person. Dio gives

us part of the official explanation : but one can easily read
between the lines.

IV

Claudius received the dispatch in Rome and set off on the
long journey by sea, road, and river to join the legions waiting for him by the Thames. About the composition of the
force he took to Britain, and indeed the route followed, our
sources are tantalizingly incomplete. A detachment of the
Praetorian Guard, under their commander Rufrius Pollio,
must have accompanied the emperor in the field. To do so
was their duty, but here there is something more. The Praetorians, two years earlier, had placed Claudius on the
throne; now they were to see him win the military glory
expected from a prince of the line of Drusus and Germanicus. And then there were the elephants, whose presence is
attested by Dio. They are more likely to have been for cere-
monial than military purposes : the 'elephant corps' of Collingwood seems wide of the mark.[23] What one would like to
know is whether Claudius brought reinforcements for the
legions and auxiliaries already in Britain. If so, the obvious
source of supply was from the Rhine armies : this consideration has a bearing on his possible route. Unfortunately none
of the ancient authorities has anything to say on this point.
Their attention is concentrated on the many distinguished
senators who were invited to follow in Claudius' retinue as
comites Caesaris. To receive such an invitation was not
necessarily a mark of honour, for the company included, besides men whom the emperor delighted to honour, others
whom he was afraid to leave behind. To this latter group
belonged that ambitious and enigmatic figure, the Gallic
senator Valerius Asiaticus. He had been a candidate for
emperor at the death of Gaius : Claudius was later to en-
compass his death and revile his memory. Then there was
Marcus Crassus Frugi, married to a descendant of Pompey,
'a man silly enough to be a possible emperor', in Seneca's

trenchant phrase. For the moment Claudius was bent on conciliating this illustrious house; Crassus' son, Cn Pompeius Magnus, had married Claudius' daughter Antonia, and was also included in Claudius' retinue. (The father was executed in AD 46, the son too came to a bad and unedifying end.) Others were M Vinicius (consul in AD 30 and again in 45), the husband of Claudius' niece Julia, and perhaps Sentius Saturninus, whose equivocal role at the time of the assassination of Gaius we have already noted. Junius Silanus, betrothed to the infant Octavia, belonged to what has been called 'the family party', as did Plautius Silvanus Aelianus, related both to the emperor and to Aulus Plautius. On Claudius' personal staff were his doctor, Xenophon, and the eunuch and freedman Posides, who presumably served as secretary in charge of the imperial correspondence.

For the progress of the invasion of Britain, the most important of these *comites Caesaris* was the future emperor, Servius Sulpicius Galba. Rich and powerful, a connection of the Empress Livia, he was now aged forty-six, and had become the trusted adviser of Claudius. As Governor of Upper Germany under Gaius and Claudius he had been outstandingly successful, crushing German attacks on Gaul in AD 40, and winning a victory over the warlike Chatti in 41. These successes were due to his qualities as a disciplinarian as well as commander in the field : he devised stiff programmes of training for the recruits to his army, and set an example of personal fitness and devotion to duty. As the man with the most recent experience of warfare in northern Europe, he would be well qualified to act as Claudius' adviser in his British command, and to make an independent assessment of the military situation. Suetonius, our sole authority for Galba's presence in Britain, refers to it in an oblique manner which has given rise to misunderstanding :
'... so high was his standing with Claudius, that, when he was afflicted by a sudden but by no means dangerous illness, the date of the British expedition was postponed'.[24] How is this to be taken? A postponement of the whole project from

an earlier year to AD 43? A postponement of the sailing of
the force under Aulus Plautius? Better than either, we suggest, a postponement of the sailing of Claudius' own 'expedi-
tio' from Boulogne : reasons of time and space alike make
this the best context for Galba's sudden but not dangerous
illness.

The route followed by the imperial expedition reflects
Claudius' interest in water transport. From Rome it proceeded down the Tiber to Ostia, soon to be the scene of a
magnificent scheme of harbour improvement. The next
stage, by sea to Massilia, was a most uncomfortable one, due
to severe gales. Suetonius [25] records that the emperor was
twice nearly shipwrecked – once off the Ligurian coast and
again off the Iles d'Hyères. The reader is always left to sift
for himself the serious from the trivial in Suetonius. This is
more than gossip. Suetonius is at pains to emphasize that the
storms were caused by the 'circius' – the swirling wind, that
dry, cold, catabatic wind known in Provence as the mistral,
so harrying to the nerves of the inhabitants of the Rhône
Valley, and destructive of shipping in the Gulf of Lyons. It
was famous in antiquity, and Augustus built it a temple, on
the basis of what experiences we do not know. But if Claudius'
encounters with the mistral had resulted in the loss of that
distinguished passenger-list, how different Roman history
would have been! No Nero, no Year of the Four Emperors ... But in fact Marseilles was safely reached, and they
began the journey across Gaul. If Marseilles was the port of
entry, Boulogne was certainly the port of exit. But what was
the route followed? Authorities differ ; Suetonius says that
Claudius marched north to Boulogne; Dio that he went
'partly by land and partly by river to the Ocean ...' There
need not be a contradiction : in any case, the more specific
statement of Dio is perhaps to be preferred. And, if so, which
rivers were used? A glance at the map would suggest the
Rhône from Marseilles to Lyons and thence by the Saône –
but to travel against the current of the Rhône does not make
for speed. Besides, Dio's words strongly suggest that the

rivers in question flowed into the Channel or the North Sea. The Rhine is the most likely of these northern rivers, and one begins to think of the great road, built by Claudius, from Andematunnum in Central Gaul to Bonna (Bonn) on the Rhine. Embarkation would be possible at Bonn itself, or even at Trier on the Moselle : near the mouth of the Rhine use could be made of Drusus' canal for a quick connection to the North Sea. More circuitous than the direct overland route to Boulogne, such a journey would enable Claudius to show himself to the armies along the Rhine, and to pick up reinforcements as he went. Or they might have been brought by Galba to some such rendezvous as Bonn, Neuss, or Cologne. But these arguments are inconclusive, and must not be pressed. Whatever route was followed, the port of embarkation for Britain was Boulogne.

'The Channel crossing was uneventful.' The words are those of Suetonius, and one may fairly read into them the wholly understandable relief of those who made the voyage. If the Roman sea (*mare nostrum*) had treated Claudius with such disrespect, what might not be expected of Oceanus himself? But no : this, the eighth crossing of the English Channel by a Roman armada, was the smoothest to date. We are nowhere told where they landed in Britain, and this has led to conjecture. But surely the only possible place is Rutupiae, where anchorage, supplies, and barracks for the troops were all in a state of readiness? Here, we may be confident, the soil of Britain was for the first time trodden by a Roman Emperor.

It would be gratifying if we could give a date for this historic occasion with even the degree of accuracy possible in the case of Caesar's first expedition. In 55 BC, Caesar anchored off Dover about 9.00 on a day in late August – probably the 26th. For Claudius a much greater margin of error must be allowed. Aulus Plautius' message – whether sent by some signal system or by courier we do not know – could have taken up to a week to reach Rome. The storms in the Mediterranean suggest at least a week for the voyage from Ostia to Marseilles : anything from three weeks to a month must then be allowed for the imperial party to cross Gaul. In short, if we suppose that Plautius sent his message in the first half of August, the imperial presence cannot have graced Britain much before mid-September. Very little of the campaigning season was left, and there would be anxiety to get back to the Continent before the 'equinoctial gales' whose existence was so firmly credited. Here lies the explanation for Claudius' short stay of only sixteen days in Britain.

It is tempting to ask what use Aulus Plautius made of August and early September, and hard to believe that he spent it, as Dio says, 'guarding what he had won'. Two possibilities suggest themselves, on indirect evidence. The fact that Verulamium was given municipal status by the Romans and that it was an object of especial hatred to Boudicca's rebels, suggests that, about this time, a section of the Catuvellauni went over to the Romans. Was this the fruit of negotiations in which, perhaps, Adminius may have had a hand? The second arises from Suetonius' statement that the victories of Vespasian's campaign in the south-west were gained 'partly under the command of Aulus Plautius, partly under that of Claudius'.[26] Now if Claudius was in Britain for sixteen days only and Vespasian's expedition was already under way, it follows that the arrangements for mounting it must have been undertaken by Aulus Plautius during this period of waiting for the Emperor. If these suggestions are accepted, it would seem that he did not waste his time. Only in two sectors were the enemy still in the field – on the approaches to Camulodunum, and in the lands of the Durotriges and the western Belgae. The second was now the major threat, and Vespasian would have it in hand. The forces defending Camulodunum could be relied upon to provide enough – but not too much – opposition for the imperial commander-in-chief.

Dio is the authority for the statement that Claudius took over the command from Aulus Plautius on the Thames. For the events that followed there is a direct conflict of evidence between him and Suetonius. Dio, as will be seen from Appendix I, speaks of a river crossing, a victorious battle against the Britons beyond the Thames, the capture of Camulodunum, and possibly a further period of fighting, resulting in the surrender of 'many British tribes'. Suetonius is emphatic that 'no battle or bloodshed' preceded the surrender of 'a portion of the island'. At first sight the statement of Josephus seems to reinforce Suetonius, for he says that Vespasian had 'by his military genius added Britain, a land previously unknown, to the Empire, thus affording Claudius ... a triumph without any exertion on his own part'. But Josephus' purpose is to flatter Vespasian at all costs: not only does he disparage Claudius, but omits any reference to Aulus Plautius and to the Medway battle. Moreover Suetonius himself says that a pageant of the sacking of Camulodunum was later enacted on the Campus Martius, which makes it clear that some British resistance must have been encountered.[27] We have no means of knowing how serious it was, nor under whose leadership. Togodumnus was dead; Caratacus, presumably, already in the west. The sixteen days spent by Claudius in Britain obviously leave no time for a campaign, but there is no need to reject Dio's statement that actions were fought in which Claudius received from his troops the tribute of being hailed as 'Imperator'. And if they departed from established form in so hailing him 'more than once in the same war', it was by no means the only such departure in that remarkable reign.

There can be little doubt that the ceremonies to be staged in the enemy capital were the real objective of the imperial presence. No description survives, but it is clear from the inscription on the Arch of Claudius and from Dio that they must have taken place. They are to be compared with the 'Durbars', as they have been called, held on more than one occasion by Julius Caesar in Gaul. Their object would be to overawe the British kings and notables by a display of Roman majesty, and to instruct them in the obligations they would have to meet once the province of Britannia was established. We can assume that they were carefully planned. The elephants – a thoughtful touch – were there for the triumphal entry into Camulodunum. Whatever the demeanour of Claudius himself (and his *bêtises* on formal state occasions were notorious and mercilessly recorded), they at least would lend dignity to the occasion.

But the most impressive ceremony must have been the formal surrender of the British kings, in the presence of the Emperor and his retinue, the Praetorian Guard, Aulus Plautius, and high officers of the invading force. This must have been a spectacle to efface memories of the court of 'the radiant Cymbeline'. According to the inscriptions on the arches at Rome and Cyzicus, eleven British kings 'formally placed themselves under the sway of the Roman people' (see Appendix III). Claudius later received a free hand from the Senate to conclude such agreements as he thought necessary in Britain, and here he effectively gathered the fruits of both war and diplomacy. We can identify some, but not all, of the British eleven. An attempt to do so in some detail is made in Appendix III (p. 165). Certainly they will have included the rulers of the three client-kingdoms now set up among the Brigantes, the Iceni and the Regnenses. Their formal act of homage completed the first phase of the invasion. The Belgic power was shattered and the groundwork of the Roman province laid. But the next phase was to prove slower, more costly and more difficult than may have been foreseen in the plan.

A special session of the Senate was held immediately the news of Claudius' British victories was announced in Rome by his messengers, Cn Pompeius Magnus and Lucius Junius Silanus. They were chosen for this mission as the sons-in-law of Claudius, and so the most suitable representatives of the imperial house. There is piquancy in the fact that the descendant of Pompey the Great, recently permitted to renew that famous name, should announce to the Senate that the work of Julius Caesar in Britain had been fulfilled – or should one say excelled? It would have appealed to Claudius, who combined *pietas* and a feeling for history with a highly individual sense of humour. Nor would it have been lost on the Senate. The honours which were then accorded to Claudius, his wife, and his son had presumably been decided in advance. For Claudius, a triumph and the erection of two triumphal arches, one in Rome and the other on the Channel coast – perhaps on the precedent of the three arches granted to Germanicus in AD 23 in Rome, on the banks of the Rhine and on Mt Amanus in Syria. For Claudius and his son, the title of Britannicus : in the same way, the title of Germanicus had been conferred on the elder Drusus and his male descendants. For Messalina, the seat of dignity that Livia had been granted, and the privilege of using the *carpentum*, the two-wheeled car used by Vestal Virgins and high officials on state occasions. Thus early in the reign appear those tendencies which, as Charlesworth has said, transformed the household of Claudius into something like a royal family.[28]

The triumph itself was held in 44, on a most lavish scale.[29] It was, after all, the first celebrated by a reigning *Princeps* since the triple triumph of Augustus in 29 BC – more than seventy years earlier. As an exceptional measure, the governors of provinces were permitted to leave their posts and come to Rome for the occasion. So, too, were certain exiles, but we are not told whether this exercise of the Imperial *clementia* went as far as a full amnesty. Suetonius and Dio comment on some of the more remarkable features of the ceremony. Claudius himself gave an exemplary display of old-fashioned *pietas* when he ascended the steps of the Capitoline temple on his knees – as Julius Caesar had done – supported by his sons-in-law. Messalina in her *carpentum* followed the triumphal chariot. Behind, on foot (following the precedent established by Augustus), came the commanders on whom the *triumphalia ornamenta* were to be conferred. They included the future Emperor Vespasian, fresh from his successful campaigns in south-west Britain, and Gn

Hosidius Geta, who had done good service at the Medway battle. M Crassus Frugi, receiving *triumphalia ornamenta* for the second time, was allowed the privilege of riding on horseback. Among others who had served in Britain were the future Emperor Galba – whose illness had caused Claudius to postpone his departure from Rome – and Vespasian's elder brother Flavius Sabinus. The comment that Claudius was unusually lavish in distributing honours seems unwarranted on this occasion. Literary sources, papyri, and inscriptions add a few other details to what is known of the triumph. *Aurum coronarium*, the gold wreaths sent by cities and provinces, was clearly on a lavish scale. Pliny singles out those from Gaul and Spain, but unfortunately the text is doubtful where he gives the figures for their weight. Other wreaths were contributed by guilds and corporations, and we have the text of the letter of acknowledgement sent by Claudius to the Guild of Travelling Athletes. An inscription from Pisidian Antioch records the decorations bestowed on P Anicius Maximus, *praefectus castrorum* of the IInd Legion *ob bellum Britannicum*, presumably on this occasion.[30] One should also take note of a group of eight poems in the Latin Anthology, all of which commemorate the Claudian invasion, and were presumably written for the triumph.[31] As *vers d'occasion*, they have a value of their own, for the business of a poet laureate, actual or would-be, is to say the obvious and say it well. We may expect them, then, to stress those features of the Claudian invasion which attracted most public comment, and in the way the government desired – to versify the headlines, as it were. What those features were is best seen in number 426 – a poem of quality, which ought to be better known :

> *Semota et vasto disiuncta Britannia ponto,*
> *cinctaque inaccessis horrida litoribus,*
> *quam pater invictis Nereus velaverat undis,*
> *quam fallax aestu circuit Oceanus,*

*brumalem sortita polum, qua frigida semper*
*praefulget stellis Arctos inocciduis,*
*conspectu devicta tuo, Germanice Caesar,*
*subdidit insueto colla premenda iugo.*
*aspice, confundat populos ut pervia tellus;*
*coniunctum est, quod adhuc orbis et orbis erat.*

The poet speaks first of Britain herself : her remoteness 'set apart in the boundless ocean'; her inaccessible shores (an echo, this, of Julius Caesar's experiences, though Claudius had found a good harbour at Richborough); the treacherous tides (another echo of Julius Caesar); the wintry climate, and the chilly, never-setting Bear that rules the British skies. Then the speed of the Claudian conquest : 'she surrendered as soon as she saw you, Caesar' – for Claudius was only in Britain for sixteen days. Finally, the reflection that there are no barriers left, and that what were once two separate worlds are joined into one. 'The world is small', said Christopher Columbus; the conquest of Britain seems to have produced in the Roman world the same feeling of barriers down. The other poems do not add much to the repertory of themes. From a reading of the poems as a whole, three leading motifs emerge, the conquest of the Ocean, the lightning campaign of Claudius, and the enlarged horizons now that the remote, mysterious island is brought into the Roman world.

Before looking at the inscription from the Arch of Claudius, together with what else is known of that monument, it is worth considering, in its completed form, the grand design for the architectural commemoration of Claudius' British victories.[32] It begins on the Palatine, where on the gable of the Imperial Palace were placed the spoils won from the enemy, the civic crown, and next to it, the naval crown 'the sign of the crossing and, as it were, the conquest of Ocean'. This was done immediately after the return of Claudius to Rome in the autumn of 43. But the main monument, the Arch of Claudius in Rome, was not dedicated until 52. Its site was carefully chosen. Standing in the Via Lata, it bridged the great artery (now the Corso) leading from the Forum and Capitol to the Porta Flaminia and the road to the north, to Gaul and to Britain itself. It was also a clever choice in terms of the topography of Rome. For this part of the Campus Martius had been developed by Augustus and was dominated by great buildings and monuments associated with him. A little farther along the Via Lata was the Ara Pacis, farther still, the Mausoleum of Augustus. The Arch of Claudius itself carried a branch of the Aqua Virgo (restored by Claudius after the neglect of Gaius) to the Pantheon and the Thermae of Agrippa, the work of Augustus' great minister. Thus the siting of the Arch of Claudius proclaimed his British conquests *Urbi et Orbi*, and brought him into association with Augustus. On the shores of the Channel, reached by a network of roads of Claudian construction, stood another triumphal arch dedicated by the Senate 'at the point whence he had set sail'. There can be no doubt that this was Gesoriacum (Boulogne), whose harbour Claudius had enlarged to make it the most important port on the North Sea. The date of the dedication of this arch is unknown and nothing of it survives. But it is not fanciful to suppose that it was built, not simply to commemorate Claudius' departure from the mainland, but as a deliberate counter to the equivocal monument of Gaius, at once lighthouse and 'trophy'. Claudius had done more than gather shells. The arch at Gesoriacum commemorated an authentic victory, and in the traditional Roman manner. Finally, there was the Temple of Claudius at Camulodunum, the royal seat of Cunobelinus and the capital of the *regnum Britanniae*; the scene, too, of the surrender of the British kings. It was intended to mark the permanence of Roman rule in Britain; Boudicca and her followers were right in regarding it as 'the citadel of eternal slavery'.

It has been shown that the four honorific inscriptions to members of the Imperial House imply that the arch of Claudius is to be compared to the Arch of Augustus at

Pavia, with its inscription to eight (or nine?) members of the Julian House.[33] Moreover, the representation on the coinage issued in AD 46, 49, 50 and 51, of an arch crowned by an equestrian statue between two trophies may well refer to this arch (*12*). Though the conquering rider is absent from Roman art of the first century AD, except for the Arch of Drusus, it accords well enough with Claudius' *pietas* that he should have taken that arch as a model. A large part of the dedicatory inscription is preserved in the courtyard of the Conservatori Museum in Rome. Its interpretation raises several problems, which are discussed in Appendix III p. 165).

# 4 Aulus Plautius and the Shaping of a British Province
## AD 43–47

I

On his departure from Britain, says Dio, Claudius 'deprived the conquered of their arms and handed them over to Plautius, bidding him also to subjugate the remaining districts'. Which were the remaining districts, and what exactly was the task assigned to Aulus Plautius? Tacitus' remark that 'the nearer part of Britain was gradually reduced into the shape of a Roman province'[1] is of some help though strictly speaking it covers the governorship of Aulus Plautius and that of his successor Ostorius Scapula. Plautius' share in this programme can be deduced from what he is known to have accomplished. When he left Britain in AD 47 the recalcitrant tribes of the south-west had been reduced by Vespasian, and a *limes* had been established which ran from the Bristol Channel by way of the lower reaches of the Severn, the Warwickshire Avon, and the Trent, to the Humber. In political terms this made a province out of the old empire of Cunobelinus, with most of the territory of the Dobunni, Durotriges and Coritani. A modern geographer would see it as the subjugation of the lowlands of Britain as far as the western edge of the limestone belt that stretches from Mendip to the Lincoln Wolds. In terms of contemporary social and economic planning, we may see in it an early version of the plan for the south-east. The military phase of this operation was a triple advance into the interior of the island : first, Vespasian's campaigns in the south-west, ending probably at Exeter : second, along the line of Watling Street into the Midlands, perhaps to High Cross : the third, northwards to Lincoln and the Humber. Once these objectives were obtained, a network of strategic roads and forts had to be constructed. In the Midlands, where potentially hostile peoples lay beyond the Severn and Trent, this took the form of a defensive zone which is implied in the construction of a Roman *limes*. Vespasian's campaign in the south-west was probably very rapid. There is evidence from some of the hill-forts that the strengthening of their defences was interrupted. The suggestion in the first edition that Vespasian went to Rome to receive his honours at the triumph of AD 44 has been seriously challenged.[2] The award was made by the Senate and did not require his personal attendance. But we do not know how long Vespasian had served with *Legio* II *Aug* before he came to Britain and his term of office may have been completed after the season of 44. No timetable can be given for the other two campaigns, nor indeed is it known whether any fighting was involved. Very probably the Roman troops, as so often, were employed as engineers rather than as combatant soldiers. Their training fitted them equally well for such tasks, and from Trajan's Column we can see how much of the time of troops in the field was devoted to the cutting of wood and turf, the siting and construction of forts and signal-stations, the gathering and transport of food and supplies. (*16, 17*)

II

We begin, then, with the drive to the south-west. It has been suggested above that it was probably launched before Claudius' arrival in Britain : also, that it was a land-sea cam-

paign, starting perhaps from Chichester harbour. The
historical evidence comes from the life of Vespasian by
Suetonius Tranquillus, in which he says : 'On the accession
of Claudius, Vespasian was indebted to Narcissus for the
command of a legion in Germany : and proceeded to Britain
where he fought thirty battles, subjugated two warlike tribes
and captured more than twenty *oppida*, besides the Isle of
Wight.' [3] This places the commander and his legion, the IInd
*Augusta*, firmly in the south-west and committed to a serious
campaign. It is doubtful whether the other parts of England
being occupied at that time would have offered so great a
resistance, and it seems to have been hardly by chance that
Vespasian was chosen by Plautius for the toughest assignment. He had shown his ability in the Medway battle and
rewarded Plautius for the confidence placed in him. While
most of the British tribes had by this time capitulated – either
by Roman persuasion in advance or by their own recognition
of the superiority of Roman arms – it is clear from archaeological evidence that the Durotriges of Dorset and Somerset
remained implacably hostile and that their strongholds had
to be taken by storm one by one.

The second conquered tribe must be either the Belgae or
the Dumnonii (as they were later called), to the north and
the west of the Durotriges respectively. There is as yet little
direct evidence to decide between them.[4] The excavations in
1934–5 at Hembury, a hill-fort just in the Dumnonian area,
produced Roman pottery of Claudian date and a Claudian
coin, and it was shown that at a late date in the fort's history part of the defences was destroyed by fire and the ramparts slighted.[5] At Worlebury, a hill-fort in Somerset overlooking the Bristol Channel, eighteen skeletons were found
with signs of battle wounds, also there was evidence of destruction and slighting, and early Roman coins,[6] but the evidence is as yet insufficient for any conclusions to be drawn.
Mention might here be made of the remarkable hoard of
horse-gear brought up by the plough at Polden Hill, near
Bridgwater in Somerset, in 1800.[7] This barbaric array, its

glittering enamels dulled by decay, suggests a wealthy British horseman.

The term 'Belgae' may have been a convenient one for the Roman authorities when marking out the boundaries of the tribes in the establishment of provincial government. This would probably have meant the grouping together of a number of small tribes with a common ethnic background whose names have been lost. The earliest coinage of this area has been shown to be derived from the Atrebates [8] to the east, and the suggestion is made that this was due to a westward movement of a section of the Atrebates loyal to the memory of their dynastic head Commius, who fled from Caesar vowing he would never look a Roman in the face again. This tribal movement must have taken place after the skilful diplomacy of Augustus had won them over to form the main pro-Roman element in Britain. Those who rejected this change of loyalty joined the western branch which may have already spread in this direction.[9] If there is any substance in this interesting theory it would imply that anti-Roman feeling might have led to active hostility in concert with the Durotriges. On balance one would favour the western Atrebates, rather than the Dumnonii, as the second warlike tribe.

About the attitude of the Durotriges there can be no doubt. Their great fortress of Maiden Castle near Dorchester was the scene of a large-scale excavation in 1934–7 by Sir Mortimer Wheeler.[10] The investigation of this most imposing of all British hill-forts produced important conclusions about the people who lived there. It was suggested by Wheeler that the multiplicity of ditches and ramparts was due to the introduction of sling-warfare into Britain, and he looked to the source of this in the defeat of the Veneti of Brittany by Julius Caesar in 56 BC. Some of these tribesmen, he suggested, fled to Britain and established themselves in Dorset. Wheeler never regarded his work at Maiden Castle as completed, and it was unfortunate that the last war prevented any further steps to bring this suggested chronology and its implications to a satisfactory conclusion. Nevertheless a further important stage was reached with the publication of the *Hill-forts of Northern France* in 1957,[11] the result of excavation and field-work intended to establish the cultural connection between Brittany and Dorset. It is evident that these explorations, while illuminating the problems of the Iron Age in north-western Gaul, in fact failed to produce the necessary links. Even so, it has only been in recent years that Wheeler's views have been seriously challenged,[12] and current opinion is that the history of the Durotriges is longer and more complicated than originally supposed.

The origins and level of prehistoric cultures can often be judged by their pottery and metalwork. Durotrigian pottery has distinctive characteristics [13] but appears to be derived from several different sources. At the time of the Roman conquest, many of the Early Iron Age forms still persisted. But the wheel had been introduced, and a group of the latest native pottery at Maiden Castle consisted of fine bead-rim bowls with an almost lustrous surface, suggesting that the potters may have been imitating metalwork. Belgic influence is marginal, and there is nothing to suggest that the Durotriges had been Belgicized to the same degree as the Dobunni. Some indication of the extent of Durotrigian territory can be gained from the distribution of their pottery types, which matches quite well the evidence of the coins. The coinage seems to have originally derived from a Gallic type brought into Britain along the south coast by settlers early in the first century BC; later it developed into distinctive local forms.[14] Unfortunately none of the Durotrigian coins are inscribed, with the possible exception of the two unusual examples bearing the enigmatic letters 'CRAB'.[15] While the precise function of such coins in the Celtic economy is not understood, it seems clear from the distribution of their find spots that they do not stray in large numbers from a well-defined area. This concentration [16] in the case of the Durotriges shows boundaries to the east on the River Avon, to the north the River Wylye, and to the west the River Axe, thus including the whole of Dorset with parts of Wiltshire and possibly Somerset and east Devon. The eastern frontier may even extend to the River Test which flows into Southampton Water. But the area between the Test and the Avon is the New Forest which has so far yielded little archaeological evidence of this period, and is hardly likely to do so in its present condition.

Of all the great hill-forts of Britain those of Wessex are the most impressive by their sheer size and complexity. They usually occupy a hill-top position, with the encircling ramparts and ditches cut along the contours. Excavations show that in many cases these sites have a long and complex history, often starting with a small fairly simple type of defence, such as a single ditch and bank reinforced with timber. Towards the end of the Iron Age much larger areas are enclosed, with several sets of ditches, and the entrances become almost labyrinthine. The ditches and banks, often cut on a steep slope, were formed by excavating the ditch and heaping the spoil on either or both lips, according to the nature of the ground. Where necessary the fronts were revetted in timber, stone, or a combination of both. Sometimes, as at Maiden Castle, the construction is of the *glacis* type, ie the slope of the ditch is continued up the bank without a break. On the south side of this great hill-fort there are four banks and three ditches spanning a horizontal distance of about 450 feet. Even today, in their slighted and weather-worn state, they present an impressive obstacle. But the most extraordinary features of these defences are the gateways. The entrances are so designed that all approaches to the final gap in the rampart are by an oblique, circuitous route overlooked the whole way by the cliff-like banks. The exact purpose of this remarkable defence in depth is not clear. At one time it was attributed simply to the introduction of the sling. As the attackers toiled up and down these obstacles they would be under attack from slingers from above who would have the advantage of height. The large piles of sling stones found on these hill-forts are evidence of this method of defence, but the explanation cannot be so simple. The bank and counterscarp normally create dead ground where attackers could lie and rest before the next rush; slingers stationed on the top of the innermost bank would only have them as targets for part of the time. There must have been some arrangement for defenders to occupy a more advanced position so that they could engage the enemy more closely – especially at the entrances – though to do so a means of easy retreat would have been needed. In this respect the native works differ from the Roman defences, where everything is controlled from the rampart top from which the entire ditch system is under direct line of fire.

These Iron Age defences may have been adequate in inter-tribal warfare. Against the organization and equipment of the Roman Army they were of little avail. There is no evidence from any of the British hill-forts to suggest that they withstood direct assault for very long. If this had failed, the Army would have settled down to a siege and thrown round the whole fortress a great circumvallation, which would have left its traces. They would then have pressed forward a series of attacks with specially designed engines and battering rams. The Romans regarded themselves as supreme in this type of warfare. Julius Frontinus, an eminent general and a later Governor of Britain, in his Introduction to Book III of his *Stratagems*, stated rather complacently that 'the invention of engines of war [for siegecraft] has long since reached its limit and I see no further hope of improvements in the applied arts ...'. What the Roman Army could do when fully extended is vividly illustrated in the account of the siege of Jotapata in AD 67, as given by Josephus (*Bellum Judaicum*, III, 141–339). The passage deserves to be read as a whole : besides its merits as a military narrative, there is the added interest that it is written by the Jewish comman-der, and that his Roman opponent was none other than Ves-pasian, now, in Josephus' words, 'grown grey in the service of Rome'. Here only the briefest summary can be attempted. Jotapata, the modern Jefat, was a position of immense natural strength, since the town was surrounded by precipitous cliffs on three sides, and strongly fortified on the fourth. Vespasian surrounded it by a double line of infantry and an outer ring of cavalry. Next archers and slingers were used to clear away all Jewish resistance outside the walls : but repeated sallies by the defenders led to five days of indecisive fighting. Then the Romans constructed earthworks opposite the fortifications of the town : this completed, they brought up 160 pieces of artillery and opened fire on the defenders. 'Simultaneously, the catapults discharged their bolts, stones of 100-lb weight were hurled by the stone-projectors, there was a hail of firebrands and of arrows. As a result, not merely were the Jews driven from the ramparts, but the whole area behind them was untenable if it came within range ...' But Jewish counter-attacks drove the Romans from their firing-position, while fatigue parties working day and night raised the height of the wall by sixty feet. Vespasian now settled down to a blockade, relying on lack of water to force the Jews to surrender. This did not happen without much further fighting, culminating in a Roman night assault combined with an appalling artillery bombardment. At last, after forty-seven days of siege, an attack delivered in the darkness before dawn and led by the future emperor Titus carried the citadel, and the town was lost. A general massacre followed. The total casualties in the siege are given as 40,000.

Operations on this scale were of course not called for in Britain : indeed, in their complexity of technique they exceed anything employed by Caesar in the war against Vercingetorix. It is unfortunate that no historian describes in detail the capture of a British hill-fort. Little help can be got from Caesar's account of the sieges of Gergovia and Alesia in Gaul, where vastly greater numbers were involved on both sides. The immensely strong natural position of Uxellodunum (Puy d'Issolu) was a last-ditch stand by 2,000 desperate men. It fell because the Romans succeeded in depriving the Gauls of access to water. It is unlikely that Vespasian ever needed this ultimate weapon. An account by Tacitus [17] of one of Germanicus' battles gives an idea of a method likely to have been used against the hill-forts of Wessex. The key position was a broad earthwork 'built by the Angrivarii to divide their lands from the Cherusci'. The German infantry were stationed on this earthwork. The Roman legionaries at first found it impossible to carry the position by assault, for, says Tacitus, 'scaling the earthwork was like trying to climb a wall, and the troops were seriously harassed from above. Germanicus saw that at close quarters the odds would be heavily against him, so the legions withdrew a short distance and two kinds of slingers were advanced to discharge their missiles and dislodge the enemy. The artillery fired bolts : the more the defenders exposed themselves, the more readily they were wounded and brought down.' It was in fact, Roman control of artillery fire of various calibres that made it impossible to defend the Celtic hill-forts. The *catapultae* could direct heavy and continuous fire against key-points, such as gateways and defended entrances. Josephus gives some impression of the terrifying effects of a Roman bombardment. A heavy stone from a Roman engine knocked off the head of a Jewish soldier : it was found three furlongs away. The noise and crash of the missiles were interminable. The more mobile slingers could quickly break up smaller concentrations along the walls. By now the way would be clear for the legionaries to advance to a spot selected for assault. No doubt they often employed the famous *testudo* or 'tortoise' formation, where the legionaries locked shields over their heads. The *testudo* was not without its troubles against a fortified city. Thus at the siege of Cremona we find the defenders harassing the *testudo* with large stones and poles and even – a heart-warming moment surely – toppling down a *ballista* on to it. At Jotapata the defenders made good use of boiling oil – without, however, halting the Roman assault. But even if the Celtic warriors had had such resources they could not have stayed in position to use them. Superior fire-power had nullified the whole idea of the hill-fort, which was to render impregnable a single strong point.

By now the only purpose they served was to collect the fighting strength of the tribes into a series of convenient receptacles, ready for a Roman force to pick them off. Vespasian's army seems to have regarded itself as a specialist in hill-fort operations; the result must have been a sort of competition to see how quickly it could be done. During the forty-seven days of the siege of Jotapata Vespasian may have thought nostalgically of the simpler problems of the hill-forts of Wessex.

We must now attempt to identify some of the twenty hill-forts taken by Vespasian. In only four or five cases is there archaeological evidence of hill-forts attacked by the Roman Army – Maiden Castle, Hod Hill, South Cadbury, Spettisbury Rings and Ham Hill. In the first of these, the evidence took the gruesome but dramatic form of a small cemetery of warriors buried at the east gate. The twenty-eight graves had been hastily dug, and the bodies thrust in with joints of meat and mugs of liquid to sustain and refresh their souls on their long journey. Many of the bodies still bore, on skulls, spines, and other bones, evidence of the sword cuts which had dispatched them. There were twenty-three male and eleven female skeletons. Some of the extensive skull injuries are eloquent of the professional skill of the legionaries in delivering their forceful blows; though other evidence makes it quite apparent that the bodies were mutilated after death. The same soldiers were also capable of taking brutal but senseless revenge on their victims for the trouble given and losses incurred. The most striking of all this evidence comes from a body with the head of a Roman *ballista* bolt still fixed into the vertebrae. The bolt had entered the body high in the chest and travelled down and through the trunk, slicing a vertebra and coming to rest with its point projecting from the back. Maiden Castle produced details of how Roman soldiers had slighted the ramparts and gateways, pulling out and scattering massive limestone blocks to ensure that the army would not have to take this fortress again. Yet there are no signs round this imposing hill-fort of

any Roman siege works. The assault must have been swift
and decisive and it says much for the skill of the legionaries
in attacking such a seemingly difficult position.

Another hill-fort to yield evidence of a Roman attack is
Hod Hill near Stourpaine, about eighteen miles in a direct
line north-east of Maiden Castle. This site has been excavated for the Trustees of the British Museum by Sir Ian
Richmond, whose main interest was the Roman fort built in
one of the corners of the Iron Age fortress. During the course
of this work it became necessary to examine the Iron Age
hut-circles to see if the natives remained there during the
Roman military occupation. Around one of the larger huts
the excavators found a number of Roman *ballista* bolt-
heads which had been aimed at this target, perhaps a rallying point round the chieftain after the tribesmen had been
driven from the ramparts. There is evidence here also that
the work of strengthening one of the gateways was never
completed.[18]

The third hill-fort is South Cadbury, made famous by the
excavations of Leslie Alcock, 1966–70, and its association
with Arthur.[19] The work provides evidence of the presence
of the Roman Army in the form of pieces of equipment and
suggestions of temporary buildings. The vast circuit of defences had suffered serious slighting. There was ample evidence of a massacre at the South-West Gate, which included
women and children who had then been buried below the
collapse of the gate. But the situation is not so clear when all
the evidence is considered. Brooches, originally with clothing
found with the skeletons, are not Claudian but Neronian (ie
*c* 54–68) and this means that the event cannot be associated
with the Conquest period, but would seem to fit into the
context of the great revolt of Boudicca in 60. This also of
course throws some doubt on similar evidence from other
hill-forts if this dating cannot be well established.

The evidence from the fourth site is by no means as reliable but is nevertheless highly suggestive. It comes from the
single-ditched hill-fort known as Spettisbury Rings, three

miles south-east of Blandford. In 1957 the Central Dorset
Railway between Blandford and Wimborne was being constructed, and a deep cutting sliced off part of the defences
of the hill-fort. What was described as a large pit [20] would
seem more likely to have been part of the ditch, and in it
were found eighty or ninety skeletons. Some of the skeletons
showed signs of battle : one skull had a piece sliced away;
another was found with a spear-head still embedded in it.
Only parts of the objects found with the burials were recovered : these are now in the British Museum. They include lance- and spear-heads of Roman military types as well
as fragments of bronze scabbard bindings and a length of
shield binding. These finds indicate a mass burial of war
victims, and the associated remains of Roman equipment
point strongly to this as another example of the Roman
Army at work. The difference between this and Maiden
Castle is that in the latter the natives were able to give their
kinsfolk a decent though hasty burial, while at Spettisbury
there may have been a mass slaughter. There the Roman
soldiers threw the bodies into the ditch and pushed the upper
part of the rampart on top of them, as they seemed later to
have done at Sutton Walls in Herefordshire.[21] Bearing in
mind the evidence from South Cadbury, it may be that the
Spettisbury massacre belongs to a later phase too.

At Ham Hill in Somerset, famous for its fine stone, excavations by St George Gray revealed a considerable quantity
of Roman military equipment, including a large piece of a
jerkin with bronze scales,[22] now in Taunton Museum. The
site of this discovery clearly indicates the presence of a
Roman Army unit on a small plateau adjacent to the 200-
acre hill-fort. The relationship may be similar to that at Hod
Hill. It is also difficult to assess the finds of military equipment from Bilbury Rings, Wiltshire, now in the Salisbury
Museum. Only careful excavation will enable the list of hill-
forts stormed and taken at this time to be extended. Probably even Eggardon and Pilsdon fell, strong as they are – but
what of Badbury Rings, Hambledon, Rawlsbury, Weatherby

Castle, Woodbury Hill, Cadbury Castle, Abbotsbury and the group to the west at Hembury, Musbury Castle, Seaton Down, Blackbury and Woodbury Castle, Castle Neroche, to mention only the most likely? Then there are the sites to the north like Bratton Castle, Battlesbury and Sidbury. But these may have been in the territory of the Belgae and can be included only if this was the second of the 'warlike tribes' to resist Vespasian's advance. There is also the chain of hill-forts along the Mendips, which would bring the total well beyond the modest twenty of Suetonius. Of Vespasian's campaign one thing seems very clear : the speed of the advance and weight of attack took the tribes by surprise, and this is shown by the examples of extensions to defences left in an unfinished state, as at Hod Hill.

### III

Until recently there was little archaeological evidence which could be linked with any certainty to Vespasian, apart from Maiden Castle and Hod Hill. Gradually pieces of the jig-saw have come to light and traces of a pattern are beginning to emerge. The mention by Suetonius of the Isle of Wight suggests that Vespasian may have planned his advance as a combined sea and land operation. With the assistance of the fleet, it would be possible to move supplies and heavy equip-ment with greater ease than by land. There were as yet no metalled roads. The army marched and rode along wide cleared lanes across the hills and forests, where hostile tribes could wage successful guerrilla action, as they were to do later in Wales. Sea transport would require secure bases, and the south coast abounds in land-locked harbours west of Bosham. One cannot however use the modern Admiralty Pilot to interpret the conditions of the first century. Many changes have taken place in the last 2,000 years; it is ex-tremely difficult to assess the combined effects of land sinkage, marine erosion, and the growth of shingle banks, besides the large-scale dredging in Southampton Water and

Portsmouth Harbour.[23] It is not unreasonable to assume that, different in shape and size as they may have been in the first century, a succession of harbours would have been available to the light-draught Roman transports. There is a growing body of archaeological evidence for this. Many years ago a legionary helmet of mid-first-century type was dredged up in Bosham Harbour. It passed through several collections and eventually found a home in Lewes Museum.[24] An oyster shell is still fixed to the crest-knob and this is evidence of the helmet lying in estuarine waters after being lost overboard. In the Chichester Museum there is a small collection of military bronzes and pieces of equipment, formerly in the Sadler Collection, and excavations in the city have produced traces of military activity, but so far no definite structures or defences.[25] The excavation of the remarkable villa at Fishbourne has revealed the presence of granaries and other timber buildings of Claudian date below the later stone structures. These had been built round a channel at the head of the harbour. There are enough traces to suggest extensive wharfage and widening of the waterways. It was impossible to extend the area of the investigation, but it is clear that the remains uncovered are only a small part of a very large establishment. The association of equipment proves that it was a military base and the coins and pottery securely date it to the invasion period, but by c 50 the base had been given up and buildings of a different character erected.[26] With this coastal area and large landlocked harbour in the friendly hands of Rome's ally Cogidubnus, it would hardly be surprising to find that Vespasian used this as a base from which to advance.

Further evidence may come from the other great harbours, showing the fleet operating from a string of bases along the coast and bringing up supplies for the army as it marched westwards. One such base, probably a permanent one, appears to have been established at Hamworthy in Poole Harbour. The area is now a desolate waste of gravel pits and factories and any hopes of further discoveries have faded. Fortunately a local school took an interest in the site before it was completely despoiled and a few trenches produced pottery of this early date which is now in Poole Museum.[27] Another base was probably sited at Topsham in the estuary of the Exe where early pottery has been found, but nothing conclusive of military occupation.[28]

No one must forget the importance of coastal stations. One of these has been known for some time, tucked into the west end of the great Iron Age hill-fort at Abbotsbury on the Dorset coast.[29] The distinctive and precise profile and plan of the square earthwork contrasts with the earlier work on this site on the ground today and from the high watch-tower in Roman times there would have been a magnificent view of the whole sweep of Lyme Bay to the distant cliffs of Devon. Other sites along the coast have been lost through slippage at the cliff face, but there are remains of an earthwork at High Peak, west of Sidmouth, and excavations there in 1929 produced first-century pottery.[30]

Of the inland forts not a great deal is yet known. Where they have been examined in detail they appear to be permanent in character and to have been occupied into the Sixties. From their distribution it seems that a tight network of closely spaced units was made necessary by the nature of the terrain and continued hostility of its population. Only the fort at Hod Hill has been completely excavated. The British Museum contains a fine collection of objects from this site which had been assiduously gathered together by Henry Durden, a Blandford ironmonger in the last century, as they were brought up by the plough.[31] Professor Richmond was asked by the Trustees of the British Museum to direct the first excavation under their auspices in Britain which would not only provide a background to the Collection, but also constitute an essential piece of research before the site was further despoiled by ploughing. The results of his eight seasons' work show a remarkable state of affairs.[32] The very siting of a Roman fort in the corner of an Iron Age hill-fort is most unusual: the normal situation is on lower ground at river crossings. Waddon, near Beaminster, is also on a hill, and if there is a fort at Ham Hill this may be a third. The reason for these anomalous sitings is the nature of the country, the absence of sizeable rivers and the hilly, broken ground which was probably thickly wooded and prevented the army from adopting its normal methods.

The plan of Hod Hill also shows peculiarities. Instead of the usual auxiliary unit, about 500 strong, there were two different kinds of troops – legionaries, and troopers of a cavalry *ala*. There was barrack provision for six centuries of legionaries (380 men) and seven troops of cavalry (234 men) and six stables. The latter were identified by the irregular patches of stained and broken chalk in the places where animal droppings would have accumulated. Each unit had its own commander, and that of the cavalry would have been the senior. There are two houses for these officers, the larger and more elaborate clearly belonging to the cavalry *praefectus*. This arrangement of putting two different kinds of unit together in the same fort is one which had serious dangers. At a later period when the fort of Newstead in Scotland was so provided, it was necessary to build a wall between the two units and give each a separate bath-house. Only in this way could quarrels and brawling be prevented.

Other buildings which were identified include a granary with its four rows of posts to raise the floor above the ground level to allow for ventilation, and make it difficult for foraging animals to gain access. Another building was thought to have been a hospital, but on less substantial evidence. The aspect which always fascinated Richmond was the defences and he used here all his brilliant skill in excavation and interpretation to demonstrate the presence of artillery platforms at each gate and discusses their fields of fire.

The sites of the other forts in the south-west have not yet been so convincingly demonstrated. The evidence for Ham Hill has already been cited [33] and the considerable collection of equipment must indicate the presence of a fort, unless these finds are part of a cache of loot. There is a small gravel plateau near Wiveliscombe about six miles due west of Taunton which is defended by ditches and rampart. In the style of fortification and choice of site commanding the valleys debouching from the Brendon Hills, this fort is typically Roman. Unfortunately the modest excavation of 1956 produced neither pottery nor equipment to clinch the issue.[34] A fort here would fit well into the strategic pattern of advanced posts half-way between Exeter and the mouth of the Parrett. A key site is that at Lake Farm, near Wimborne Minster, Dorset. It is evident from small-scale investigations[35] that it is a large and complicated establishment which may have started as a Plautian fort.

One of the important facts which emerges from a study of early forts is that in many cases their sites later became civil settlements. The presence of troops would have attracted those natives who could see an opportunity of developing trade. Soldiers in foreign service the world over have human needs – food, drink, entertainment, women – which only civilians can supply. These transactions flourished regardless of any feelings of hostility, and small civil settlements would have sprung up outside the forts. From these modest origins would develop the permanent towns, many of which survived the later movement of troops towards the north and west. In this area there are the Roman towns of Exeter, Dorchester, Ilchester, Camerton and Sea Mills, the first two being tribal capitals. It would be a reasonable assumption that they also began in the first century as forts, and if they are seen in relationship to the known military sites they seem consistent with the general pattern. This is equally true, as will be seen below, of the forts in the rest of the frontier zone. In the south-west, too, it seems quite certain that these towns could not have had any earlier origin : but in all these examples excavations have been on too small a scale to produce much direct evidence.

Exeter suffered serious damage during the last war; excavation has preceded some of the redevelopment and the results of this work have been published.[36] The earliest levels were found to be rich in pottery and glass of the Claudian period, but devoid of military equipment. In 1964–5 the South Gate was investigated by Lady Aileen Fox with the dramatic discovery of a military-type ditch at right angles to the civil defences.[37] Claudian pottery found in the filling included at the bottom a large fragment of an amphora with the peaked handles typical of this period. But any suggestion that the fort lay so far to the south of the later Roman town centre received a setback, when work was undertaken in 1972 in the Cathedral Green in front of the west door. The significance of these remarkable discoveries will be discussed below in their proper context, but enough Claudian pottery was recovered from this and adjacent areas to postulate the presence of a fort here at the time of Plautius (see pp. 127–9). The South Gate ditch presumably belongs to a military compound perhaps connected with wharfage on the river bank nearby.

Dorchester has produced a few items of equipment, including the bone sword-handle grip of a legionary *gladius* and a very fine enamelled belt-mount (*11*).[38] Doubtless the site of the fort will be found during the excavation of the Roman town, which probably spread over it. There is no evidence as yet from Ilchester or Camerton,[39] but at the latter the early construction of the Fosse Way seems to be confirmed. There must be other forts in the area, possibly somewhere near Axminster and Yeovil, awaiting discovery.[40]

The situation along the coast-line of the Bristol Channel would have been quite different from that of the south coast, since supplies brought by sea would face the long and difficult journey round Land's End. Forts in north-west Somerset are more likely to have been supplied by land routes from the south and east. The harbours along the Channel, however, had another part to play in later campaigns. As soon as a decision was taken to wage war on the Silures of South Wales, naval bases would be needed for reconnaissance, attack and ferrying troops and supplies across the Bristol Channel. This will be discussed below in the proper context.

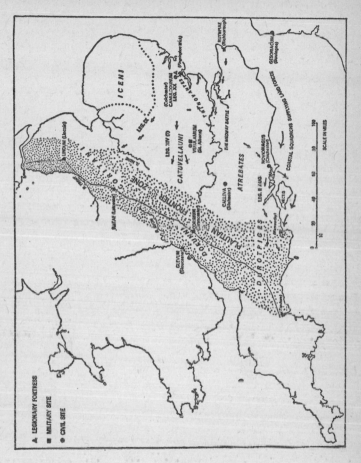

*Fig. 3: The advance under Aulus Plautius and the frontier of AD 47*

It is sufficient at this stage to note the two important harbour inlets, at Combwich at the mouth of the Parrett, and
Sea Mills at the mouth of the Avon. The sea-level here has
risen since Roman times and sites of that period are now
found below the modern sea and water-table at places like
Weston-super-Mare. Sites on higher ground will of course
remain and there is a small Roman settlement at or near
Combwich, whose late cemetery at Cannington with its
thousands of burials has been excavated in recent years.[41] It
seems possible that the Roman settlement developed outside
an early fort. On the other hand, this is an obvious site for a
small port and trading settlement. For Sea Mills there is
better evidence, recovered from rather casual digging on a
site which is now almost obliterated by housing development.[42] The early pottery, coins and military equipment are
conclusive evidence of a fort or naval base; from the small
later civil settlement, known as Abonae according to the
Antonine Itinerary, a ferry service probably operated across
the Bristol Channel.

It should be clear from this survey that the archaeological
traces of the conquest and subsequent occupation of the
south-west, although faint, are certain enough for a pattern
to be distinguished and even for some conclusions to emerge.
The gaps in our knowledge are, however, very large. Many
more discoveries are needed before we can interpret the
work of Vespasian, or understand the problems which faced
the military authorities in maintaining large forces in this
hostile area. We do not yet know how long this was necessary, nor whether the units were withdrawn at the same
time or by stages.

IV

The evidence of archaeology is the only guide for the advance to the midlands and the north since there are no bio-
graphical details of the commanders involved. Before any
forward move could be made, Aulus Plautius, that prudent

general, established a strong base in the rear at Colchester, with easy access to the sea and the mouth of the Rhine. The evidence for the army at Camulodunum appears in Tacitus, who refers to the later establishment of the *colonia* in terms to suggest that freeing a legion was its object. There are also two military tombstones found separately near Beverley Road (2, 4).[43] One is of M Favonius Facilis, a centurion of the XXth Legion, and shows in relief a grim-visaged officer holding his vine stick, a symbol of rank, with one hand, while the other rests on the pommel of his sword slung on his left. His dress and armour are seen in fine detail, down to the highly decorated belt-plate. The stone proclaims his authority and there is a clear touch of arrogance in his stance. To stand before this monument in Colchester Museum is to begin to understand something of the might of Rome, and to feel a measure of compassion for the free Celtic warriors being crushed by such assurance and efficiency. The other stone, of equal interest, is that of an auxiliary horseman, Longinus of the First Thracian *ala*.[44] He was the son of Sdapezematygus and came from Sardica, which is now Sofia in Bulgaria. He wears a jerkin of large bronze scales (*lorica squamata*), carries an oval shield and rides a well-groomed horse which strides over a naked hairy foe cowering in terror like Caliban.

Both these stones appear to have belonged to a small military cemetery along a Roman road which ran approximately from east to west, but a quarter of a mile south of the *colonia*. The two tombstones were broken and defaced by the British rebels at the time of the Boudiccan revolt in AD 60.[45] There must be somewhere, near the site of the *colonia* founded by Ostorius Scapula, a sequence of military establishments which may be very difficult to disentangle and fit into their historical contexts. First there was a base for *Legio* XX with other units also present, as well as the headquarters of the main command. A great flurry of activity would have been connected with the brief visit of the Emperor Claudius and his review of the troops and reception of the British Kings to receive their submission. The founding of the *colonia* would not have meant the end of the military base and, of course, the army returned in strength in the tragic aftermath of the great revolt. All these events must have left some mark in the ground. But until recently with the exception of a scatter of military objects [46] very little has been identified. Like most towns, Colchester has been subject to modern development and in the excavations it has been possible to recognize traces of Claudian timber buildings coming to light.[47] Most of these seem to be concentrated on the west side of the town and their plans suggest rows of barrack-blocks in a fortress of some fifty acres, the size one would expect for a legion. There is evidence from Fingringhoe,[48] which lies in the estuary of the River Colne, that this may have been the site of a military store-base with direct access to the mouth of the old Rhine, where military activity of this period has been attested.[49]

A small two-acre fort has been postulated overlooking the Thames at Orsett, near Grays Thurrock.[50] Mid-first-century features with military objects are recorded from Kelvedon which later became the site of the settlement of Canonium [51] and there is growing evidence of a large site of Claudian date under modern Chelmsford.[52]

To the south and east of the Severn and the Trent the only tribes which escaped the domination of the Catuvellauni were the Iceni of East Anglia and the Durotriges of Dorset, both of too tough and independent spirit to fall before the Belgic Kingdom. The Iceni remained independent for the time being; the implacable Durotriges were battered into surrender by the IInd *Augusta*. A section of the Dobunni to the west, as we have seen, seem to have succumbed to the Catuvellauni and were quick to ally themselves to Rome.

The position of the other midland tribe, the Coritani, is more difficult to assess. This people appear to have occupied the eastern watershed of the Trent and to have included the modern shires of Lincoln, Leicester and Rutland. If this was indeed the tribal area, the Trent seems to have been a political divide. To the east in Lincolnshire there is growing evidence of Belgic influence and the centre of this may have been Old Sleaford, where traces of a mint have been found. On the Humber at South Ferriby Belgic pottery indicates a settlement or trading-post. Beyond the Trent, apart from a few coins in Yorkshire, there are only hoards, buried perhaps by refugees or traders. The Coritanian coins [53] form a common frontier with those of the Iceni along the River Nene and extend to the south-west to the divide between the watersheds of Trent and Avon. The peoples west of the Trent appear to be a mixture of earlier cultures unaffected by Belgic influence. Pottery evidence suggests that Leicester was a pre-Roman settlement.[54] The tribe may originally have been confined to the territories east of the Trent and subject to Belgic overlords. When the Romans later organized Britain into a province the more backward tribes west of the river may have been added to form the *civitas Coritanorum*. The siting of the capital of Leicester, so far from the apparent centre of its tribal area, may have been influenced by the creation of the *colonia* at Lincoln, and perhaps by the designation of the Fens as a special development area or Imperial domain.

Aulus Plautius probably advanced into these regions from Colchester with circumspection, leaving forts in his rear. For a short time at least it was deemed prudent to have a fort at Verulamium, the old capital of the Catuvellauni. There has been found, buried underneath the town's late second-century bank but overlying Belgic occupation, a typical military rampart revetted in timber.[55] This accords with items of military equipment found in excavations in the Roman town and nearby. A legionary helmet of this early period was found in 1813 when the Grand Junction Canal was being cut at Northcott Hill.[56] A punched inscription on the neck-guard indicates that one of its owners was a legionary of the first cohort. The legion concerned is probably the XIVth, which advanced north-west along the line of Watling Street, eventually to reach Wroxeter. Mid-first-century timber buildings of military-type construction indicate a possible fort at Bow Brickhill, near Fenny Stratford.[57]

The other legion involved in the advance was the IXth. Its route may be judged by the fact that it became eventually established at Lincoln. This force, then, advanced in a northerly direction, skirting the boundaries of the Icenian kingdom and the Fens, yet to be drained. Dr St Joseph found from the air a large fort about half legionary size near Longthorpe on the Nene.[58] Excavations from 1967 to 1971 by the discoverer and Professor Frere have revealed timber buildings including the *principia* and a granary, dated by Claudio-Neronian pottery. There is a smaller fort of later date inside the larger one.[59] In an area adjacent to the fort a batch of pottery kilns has been found which were producing wares for the army. It is not clear if these are part of a military depot, or potters working under contract.[60] The whole establishment appears to have been given up by *c* 65 and the land given over to agriculture. The situation is even further complicated by an air photograph taken by Dr St Joseph which shows the defences of part of yet another fort to the west of the large one. But the pottery recovered from this area is as yet indistinguishable from the wares made nearby. There is yet another fort protecting what is presumably a later crossing of the river near the town of Durobrivae (Water Newton).[61] The river was probably the southern boundary of the Coritani, and the attitude of this tribe to the Romans may at this stage have been uncertain. It may be noted also that there is some slight evidence of a Roman fort at Cambridge in the form of a ditch yielding Claudian pottery[62] under the Shire Hall, and another at Godmanchester.[63] These may be Plautian forts in the newly conquered region – unless of course they belong to the later troubles of AD 60.

Gradually, then, the army moved into its forward area, legions and *auxilia* alike. Until the sites of more forts are known it is impossible to consider in detail the basic pattern of the new frontier created by Aulus Plautius. Up to a few years ago no one was quite sure that it even existed, but thanks mainly to air photography it is possible to glimpse the situation. The Roman governor had to deal with a problem for which there was little precedent. The main imperial frontiers laid down by Augustus had definite physical boundaries. To the west was the Atlantic, to the north the great rivers Rhine and Danube, to the east the deserts of Parthia, and to the south the greater desert of the Sahara. In regions of uncertainty, client kingdoms were set up as buffer states. Behind these lines the Roman Army was thinly stretched, but units were usually grouped together in large camps – a survival of the earlier idea of winter quarters. The method is well illustrated by Caesar's campaigns in Gaul, where after the summer campaigns the general carefully placed his legions to winter where they could be well supplied, keep an eye on the uncertain tribes, and be easily brought together in an emergency. In these winter quarters the troops bivouacked under their leather tents, and the whole arrangement was considered to be a temporary one. In the east, where there were urban civilizations older than that of Rome, the solution was easier, for the troops were merely quartered in the cities. As the frontiers became firmly established and the districts now within the Empire pacified, it was natural for the army to winter along the frontier itself. But by now the soldiers had years of bitter experience of attempting to camp out in the winters of north-western Europe. The attempts to dig drainage channels round the tents to prevent the camp from being completely waterlogged are seen at the site of Hofheim near Wiesbaden. At some period – probably under the old warrior Tiberius whose knowledge of these conditions from personal experience was greater than that of Augustus – the *hiberna* gave place to the permanent fort with its wooden barracks, stores and other buildings. By AD 43 the practice was well established and the tented camp was normally a feature only of summer campaigns. The development in the planning of internal arrangements from tents to permanent wooden buildings was still in progress, however, and presents some fascinating problems. Because tents can be easily pitched and struck the internal planning of the *hiberna* tended to be a loose affair with merely a rough division of barrack areas, horse lines, through-ways and store and waggon parks. The commander's tent was pitched in the centre and the others grouped around it. So it is hardly surprising to find in the early timber forts a lack of rigid planning. The Claudian forts in Britain show great variety, both in general planning and the internal arrangement of buildings, which makes it often difficult to offer a precise identification of each. The effect of this is to make these early forts extremely interesting to excavate and quite unlike the stereotyped planning which had become established by the end of the first century. It is possible, for example, in the forts of Agricola, to identify and plot the buildings by cutting a series of trenches across them in a reasonably economical manner; the Claudian forts require a much more extensive investigation before they can be understood.

In looking for the site of early forts there is – as we have seen – a very useful indication in the presence of a Roman civil settlement. It can only be a matter of time before forts are found at Canterbury, Winchester and Rochester.


v


Bearing this general pattern in mind, it is possible to make a tentative map of the forts in the frontier laid down by Aulus Plautius (see page 87). It soon becomes clear that it represents defence in depth in a strip of country some thirty miles wide. As suggested above, this may not so much be for protection against a frontal assault as to occupy the territories of tribes of uncertain allegiance. The forward position rests on the estuary of the Exe, the shore of the Bristol Channel, the lower Severn, the Warwickshire Avon, the Trent and the Humber. That this represents the limit of the Plautian

system is shown by the famous comment of Tacitus in de-
scribing the activities of the next Governor, Ostorius Scapula, who, when forced to advance still further, is said to have
'disarmed the suspected tribes and established control over
the area on this side [ie the Roman side] of Trent and
Severn'.[64] The road known as the Fosse Way has long been
recognized as a military conception;[65] it now appears not as
the *limes* itself, but as a lateral line of communication affording protected access to all parts of the frontier zone. One
must here accept the continuation of the same military road
north of Lincoln to the Humber, striding along the Lincoln
Edge.[66] Finds of early pottery and brooches on the Humber
shore may mean no more than trade, but one would expect
a fort in this important position to watch any movements
across the estuary. The most probable site is at Old Winter-
ingham, where Dr Ian Stead has found roads, ditches and
early timber buildings of military-type construction, all associated with a considerable quantity of pre-Flavian pottery
some of which may have been made locally.[67] There is a
cuirass hinge from a *lorica segmentata* in the Scunthorpe
Museum from Owmby and early brooches and a military
buckle have also been found there.[68]

The situation at Lincoln itself has yet to be resolved. At
one time it was believed that the hill top was occupied by
*Legio* IX from the time of Plautius. This seems to be confirmed by three tombstones of legionaires bearing only two of
the three names of a citizen.[69] The absence of the *cognomen*
has been taken to indicate a Claudian date.[70] But not only
does the discovery of the Longthorpe fort throw some doubt
on this, but the finds from Lincoln itself. Enough pottery has
been discovered from excavations of the earliest levels to
indicate that the fortress was not established until after 60.[71]
But it seems unthinkable that this important strategical position was not held by the army as soon as the region was
occupied. The Fosse Way turns a sharp angle south of Lincoln and this raises the possibility that the earliest site is in
this area on the South Common. One must surely expect one

or more forts somewhere at this period with possibly changes of location.

There are traces of military occupation along the Fosse Way, but little of it has been securely dated. At Brough, where a small settlement known as Crococalana later developed, a fine bronze cheek-piece of an auxiliary trooper's parade helmet has been found.[72] The next site to the south is Ad Pontem (Thorpe-by-Newark) where there must have been a bridge across the Trent constructed when pacification had been established. Here there is a complexity of crop-marks suggestive of defences : evidence has now been found in recent excavations of several military-type sites including what was perhaps a stores-base by the river and an earlier fort probably of Plautian date.[73] Farther along still an anomalous situation exists at Margidunum (Castle Hill),[74] where the apparent remains of a Claudian fort with internal stone buildings have been published. It now seems quite clear in the light of recent work by Mr Malcolm Todd that the area investigated was part of the civil settlement, and that the area of military activity was quite extensive but definite evidence of a fort has yet to be found.[75] Furthermore the pottery published by Dr Felix Oswald as Claudian seems in the light of re-examination more likely to belong to c AD 50–60.[76]

The situation at Leicester is bedevilled by the presence of a stamped tile now in the Museum. It appears to read LVIII in reverse, but has been taken to refer either to the Legio VIII or VIIII, on the assumption that it could have been a broken die.[77] There is some doubt about the presence of the Eighth Legion in the invasion force and it is even less likely that any detachment would have stayed here to take up permanent quarters. There is also the problem of the presence of military tile-works in Britain at this period. It was a wide-spread practice elsewhere, but there are no stamped military tiles in Britain which can be dated before the close of the first century.[78] This does not mean that the army was not using tiles; there were many found at Fishbourne associated with the Claudian store-base and if the bath-house at Exeter is c AD 50–65, its tiles would prove the existence of a large tile-works at this time. Whatever may be the truth about this tile, there are traces of the army in the city of Leicester; a decorated belt-plate was found in 1953 and there are other pieces of equipment; and a military-type ditch near the river has produced Claudian samian from its filling.[79]

There are, however, two possible fort sites in advance of the Fosse in this sector. One is where a unit might be expected to protect a crossing of the Trent – at Littleborough, four miles south of Gainsborough. A well-defined Roman road, now known as Till Bridge Lane, branches from Ermine Street and heads north, offering an alternative route to the crossing of the Humber and to York. This must have been the main Roman highway to the north in a later context. It appears in the Antonine Itinerary, and there would probably have been a bridge here at that time. This is however one of the Roman routes which has fallen into disuse – probably after the collapse of the bridge – the crossing at Gainsborough being preferred since the time of the Danes. The Roman settlement of Segelocum was established on the west bank of the Trent, but the fort is most likely to have been on the other side. Stukeley has an enigmatic note 'On the east side of the river has been a camp',[80] but whatever earthworks he may have seen or heard about have now vanished under the plough. Another possibility has been suggested by Dr St Joseph with the discovery of a 25-acre fort at Newton-on-Trent, five miles to the south [81] (see p. 157). There is another fort site at Broxstowe beyond the Trent, which is now obliterated by a council housing estate on the north-western outskirts of Nottingham. Earthworks have been noted here and some sporadic excavations, rather ill-recorded, did produce Claudian pottery and coins, and also some military equipment which was not identified at the time.[82]

There are no other known forts of this period in Lincolnshire, but the siting of the little towns at Caistor and Horn-castle suggests military planning. This may of course belong to a much later period. A fort has been postulated at Ancaster on the River Witham where a Roman town (Causennae) later developed,[83] and a ditch system found in the West Cemetery in 1965 may be considered further evidence.[84] On the two routes between Ancaster and Durobrivae there is one known fort at Great Casterton, at the crossing of the Gwash on the western limb. Here a series of summer schools, directed by Dr Philip Corder, explored the defences of the small Roman town and a villa nearby.[85] Early pottery and a piece of military equipment gave advance warning of the presence of a fort. In spite of intensive searching and discussion of the problem, it was only after the school had closed down that the fort was discovered in the field next to that in which much of the excavation had taken place. Under exceptional circumstances crop-marks had developed and Dr St Joseph observed and photographed the unmistakable outlines of two forts, one within the other.[86] Although much of this site had been open and available for excavation while the school was in operation, new bungalows were now being built across the northern part of it. Two further seasons of excavation were carried out by some of the students of the previous schools under Professor I. A. Richmond. Sufficient pottery was recovered to establish a Claudian date for the military occupation. The ditch of the reduced fort had at a later date been considerably enlarged by doubling its depth, going well into the solid limestone. Among the finds was a turf-cutter, very like one in any modern ironmonger's shop, and a fine intaglio for a ring which may have been worn by a centurion, showing the standards and an eagle. Two periods of timber buildings were clearly discernible; with work on a larger scale it would be possible to obtain the plans of the two forts in the area free of the road and modern houses.[87]

In the central part of the Fosse frontier, between Leicester and Cirencester, no military sites are known. This is prob-

ably due, as we shall see, to the fact that this sector was
vacated in AD 48–9. Even so there must have been forts in
this area; doubtless they will be found. In any attempt to
locate them the sites of the civil settlements should be the
first to be considered. High Cross (Venonae) is situated at the
junction of the Fosse Way and Watling Street and is clearly
a site of major strategic importance. A possible site was recorded by Dr St Joseph, but excavations have produced no
conclusive evidence in the form of pottery or metalwork.[88]
There is a considerable spread of civil occupation around
the junction of the Roman roads, but the pottery does
not seem to be earlier than c AD 70. The next site to the
south along Watling Street is Cave's Inn (Tripontium), but
it is unfortunate that most of the site had been removed by
gravel working before any detailed investigation could be
made. Among the many objects found during these operations is a fine military mess-tin,[89] identical with others of the
Claudian period. Much mid-first-century pottery has turned
up at Duston and Kettering[90] and this may also represent
the passage of the army – if it is not the result of earlier
Belgic intrusion. Of the other settlement sites such as Irches-
ter, Whilton Lodge (Bannaventa), Towcester (Lactodorum),
Chesterton (on the Fosse) and Dorn, so little work has been
done that it is hardly surprising that nothing has yet been
found. Alchester in Oxfordshire has been partly excavated
and produced an early type of harness clip[91] and a baldric
loop.[92]

For one of the advance posts in this sector a possible site
is Alcester on the Alne, a tributary of the Warwickshire
Avon. A harness ring with a masked loop, like those used by
an auxiliary cavalry,[93] was found in an excavation in 1938
and pieces of cavalry equipment more recently.[94] To the
north-east is the important Neronian base at The Lunt,
Baginton, near Coventry, excavated with such outstanding
success by Mr Brian Hobley.[95] To the south of this site there
have been extensive gravel workings and some of the finds
made there have been recorded. Among these is a remark-

able samian jug by the potter Sabinus, dated by J. A. Stan-
field to *c* AD 30–46.[96] If this is not a survival, it could be a
hint of earlier occupation, but the damage to the area has
been so extensive, that there seems little hope of recovering
much more evidence. The next sign of anything military is at
Mancetter (Manduessedum) on Watling Street to the north-
east. There are two quite different sites here. The Roman
town lies astride the road, while a mile away in a much
better tactical position is the small hamlet of Mancetter with
its fine church and manor house. Stukeley visited this site in
the company of the great Warwickshire map-maker Henry
Beighton and records a deeply entrenched camp 'but I cannot say with so much regularity as to its present appearance
that will ascertain it to the Romans'. In 1964, a hoard of
sixteen Claudian coins was found in digging for a drain outside the gates of the Manor [97] which suggests early occupation, but a defensive system examined in 1955 and 1969 has
been shown to be Neronian.[98] A military-type ditch has been
found by Mrs K. Hartley in excavations on the pottery
works on the other side of the river.[99]

Between the central area and the south-west, the problems of which have already been discussed, there lie the
Cotswolds and the valley of the lower Severn. A key position
must have been the junction of Avon and Severn. The best
site here is the narrow angle between the two rivers where
there is now a motte and bailey castle, showing its tactical
importance. Recent investigations in Tewkesbury itself have
produced evidence of prehistoric and Roman occupation,
but of post-Claudian date. Nine miles to the south is Gloucester, where military activity is certain. There are at least
two distinct sites, at Kingsholm to the north-east of the city,
and below the medieval city itself. The Kingsholm site has in
the past decade been much built over and large-scale investigation is no longer possible. During the early nineteenth
century much metalwork was found, probably by the
plough, and this was illustrated and discussed by that inde-
fatigable Gloucestershire antiquary Samuel Lysons.[100] These

1  The Emperor Claudius. From a bust, first century AD

2  Auxiliary cavalryman, from Longinus's tombstone, Colchester

3  A Gallic warrior

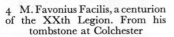

4  M. Favonius Facilis, a centurion of the XXth Legion. From his tombstone at Colchester

5  A soldier of the XIVth 'Gemina' Legion. From a tombstone at Mainz

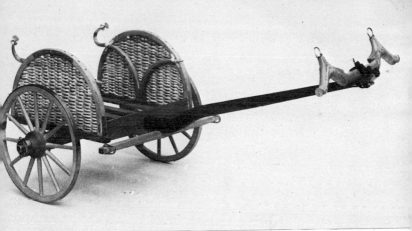

6   A reconstructed model of a British chariot

7   Celtic arms and equipment – detail of the Triumphal Arch at Orange

8 The River Medway above Rochester, at the point where the Roman
army probably fought its way across

9 A carro-ballista, a spring gun mounted on a cart. From Trajan's
Column in Rome

10 Maiden Castle in Dorset, a British Iron Age hill-fort which was
stormed and sacked by Vespasian's legion

11 A bronze belt-plate decorated with millefiore inlay, from Dorchester,
Dorset

12 Triumphal arch: Claudius's victory over the Britons (DE BRITANN [IS]). From an aureus of Claudius

13 Claudius in triumph after his British campaign. From a cameo

14 A column of the Praetorian Guard on the march. From Trajan's Column

15 Roman cavalry equipment from the Seven Sisters Hoard, Glamorgan. (See Appendix V)

16 Roman soldiers building a rampart with spoil from the ditch between turf revetments at front and back. From Trajan's Column

17 Embarking men and supplies at a port. From Trajan's Column

objects were placed in the British Museum, but time has not dealt kindly with the ironwork and little survives, although the finest item, a bronze mess-tin,[101] is still in splendid condition. There are a few more objects in the Gloucester Museum. It is not possible to identify the troops who occupied this site, though some of the equipment (such as the pioneer axe-head sheaths and what may be a *pilum*-head) was used by legionaries. The finds recorded by Lysons, and early coins and pottery since his day, together with the behaviour of the Roman road system, all strongly indicate the presence here of a unit of the army. This may, in the initial phase, have been the Thracian cohort commemorated by the tombstone of Rufus Sita now in the Gloucester Museum.[102] The XXth Legion was moved to Gloucester as a result of a situation which forms part of the later history of the frontier and is discussed below.

Another site which has received much attention of recent years is Cirencester. Progress is disfiguring this once lovely Cotswold town, the site of a large and important Roman city. The opportunity for excavation so provided has been taken by Mr John Wacher and Mr Alan McWhirr, and they have added much new material. The town has long been known to have early military connections. There are two fine cavalry tombstones in the Museum of troopers of two different auxiliary units, an *ala Indiana*[103] and an *ala Thracum*.[104] The latter is the finer of the two and shows the caparison in some detail; although his face is damaged it seems probable that the trooper was wearing a parade helmet with a face-mask and carries a standard which appears to be folded. Although the armour is quite different from that of the Colchester stone it is possible that it was the same unit : the difference may be that of rank between a standard-bearer and a trooper. A third tombstone, found near these two at about the same time, appears to be of an equally early date but commemorates a civilian, one Philus of the Sequani, a tribe in the upper Saône valley in east Gaul. This man was possibly a trader who followed in the wake of the army.[105] Among the objects found in the town, and which are now in the Museum collection, are over a dozen pieces of military equipment, some clearly belonging to the cavalry, such as the remarkable gilded chest-plate with a bird mount.[106] Until 1961, the site of the fort was a matter of speculation. In that year, however, Mr Wacher, in his excavations to west of the Basilica of the Forum, found the defences, consisting of two ditches, a turf rampart, and traces of timber buildings of three periods inside the fort.[107] A remarkably fortunate discovery was a large quantity of pottery, thrown into the inner ditch when the site was abandoned and levelled out. Surplus supplies from the quartermaster's stores were literally ditched. This helps to establish a terminal date which seems to be not earlier than c AD 60–5; but if the pottery was by then old stock and so discarded, it may be somewhat later.

Little can be said of any other sites to the south of Cirencester but it would seem possible that some of the civil settlements like Mildenhall (Cunetio), Sandy Lane (Verlucio), Wanborough (Durocornovium) [108] and White Walls may have had a military origin. So also might Bath (Aquae Sulis), as the potentialities of the hot springs were quickly developed.[109] Among the inscriptions of those who sought the waters are some belonging to soldiers, but they must be of a later period, except Vitellius Tancinus, a trooper of the *Ala Vettones* [110] and a native of Lusitania where the regiment had been raised. This suggests that he was a serving auxiliary of the invasion period. A possible fort site exists near Kingscote where military bronzes have been found on a large Romano-British settlement site.[111] There is another possibility at Nettleton Shrub in North Wiltshire.[112]

The pattern of the military frontier devised by the first Governor, Aulus Plautius, begins to take shape, although at present it is ill-defined in places. Troops have been concentrated in the forward areas but one cannot at present be certain of this, since many of the sites remained in military hands throughout the first century, and the later remains

obscure the earlier. The rest of the Province was also garri-
soned perhaps more thinly. Forts could have been established at all the British settlements, as at Verulamium; nor
were the client kingdoms exempt since Chichester had a
garrison and so apparently did Silchester. Among the vast
collection of material from the Society of Antiquities' excavations of 1890 to 1909, at the latter are rosette studs
from a *lorica segmentata* [113] found in a pit in *Insula XXIII*.
Mr George Boon has published other finds including a hinge
and hook, also from legionary body armour.[114] The presence
of a fort in the northern part of the city may have had an
effect on the layout of the later street plan as at Verulamium.[115] The situation with Iceni is still not certain as the
military sites in the territory are not dated.The great strategical importance of the Thames crossing at London must
have been recognized from the beginning and the extensive
finds of early military metal and leather work in the Wal-
brook [116] must indicate the presence of a fort nearby, nor must
one forget the fine Claudian legionary helmet from the
Thames and now in the British Museum, and the *gladius*
in its scabbard.

The Governor had reason to be satisfied with his arrangements, for he had completed in a thoroughly workmanlike
manner the task to which he had been assigned. The addition of the British lowlands to the Empire, begun so in-
auspiciously by the great Julius, was now complete. An awkward legacy inherited by Augustus was tidied up in a most
satisfactory manner. Aulus Plautius, his term of office having
expired, could retire to Rome and enjoy his *ovatio*.[117] This
'lesser triumph' was a distinction by then almost never
awarded outside the Imperial family, to which Aulus Plautius was indeed connected by marriage. A triumph for the
Emperor, but merely *triumphalia ornamenta* for victorious
generals, had become the practice. Both Claudius' anti-
quarianism and his sense of the value of Aulus Plautius'
work in Britain are attested by this revival of the *ovatio* for
a senator after an interval of sixty-six years. The attention

accorded by the Emperor in coming out of the city to meet
the returning Governor, and in conceding him the place of
honour in the ascent to the Capitol, aroused much comment.
The whole affair would have served to keep the conquest of
Britain before the public gaze.[118]

But however satisfied Claudius and his ministers may have
been at the outcome, there were others less content. The
elder Pliny records that the possibility of large new sources
of silver in Britain, of which there must have been an inkling,
caused perturbation among the owners and lessees of the
Spanish silver mines, some of which were by now becoming
very deep, and where extraction of the ore was being made
difficult by flooding.[119] Fearing a sudden reduction in the
price of silver, the proprietors of the mines attempted to
place restrictions on the British output. Although Caesar
had told Cicero that there was no silver in Britain, this may
have been an excuse for not pursuing his plans of conquest.
It may have been the development of British coinage that
started the first serious search for silver deposits, though it
seems that the Romans knew of the Mendip ores. A stamped
lead pig datable to AD 49 [120] shows that silver extraction was
in full swing five years after the landing. The fact that the
inscription on the pig includes the letters 'DE BRITAN'
suggests that the silver and lead were both exportable com-
modities; this rapid assault on the mineral wealth of Britain
implies a strong economic motive for the conquest. It is not
surprising to find at Charterhouse a small earthwork resembling a fort which has produced some Claudian
samian.[121]

# 5 Ostorius Scapula and the Campaign
in Wales AD 47–51

## I

The second Governor of Britain did not find it a rewarding
assignment. Nothing is known of the earlier career of
Ostorius Scapula. We can deduce a military reputation, but
do not know where it was gained. He held the consulship
some time earlier than AD 45. In the autumn of 47 he crossed
to Britain to find the province in a state of turmoil which he
never wholly suppressed, despite his great achievement of
defeating Caratacus in Wales.

For the campaigns against Caratacus in Wales and their
preliminaries Tacitus is the only historical source. Archaeology can offer supplementary evidence, but this, as will be
seen later, is seldom clear or precisely datable. It is therefore
important to know what limitations and conventions the use
of Tacitus must impose. His account of the Claudian invasion, and (presumably) the events in Britain under Aulus
Plautius, will have come in one of the lost Books of the
Annals. It will have told of Caratacus' movements after his
defeat at the Medway, and of the position he was able to
win among the tribes of Wales. The narrative we have[1]
carries an account of British affairs from AD 47 to 57, under

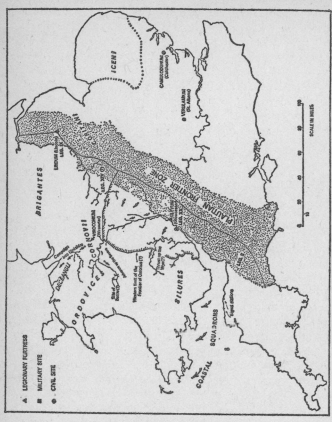

Fig. 4: The advance under Ostorius Scapula

Ostorius Scapula and Didius Gallus. The unwarlike Didius
Gallus (as Tacitus portrays him) comes only in the last of
nine chapters, and seven of the others are given over to the
Caratacus episode, which covers four years (AD 47–51).
Selective and highly compressed, much is omitted; two epi-
sodes are chosen for special treatment. These are Caratacus' final battle, and his speech at the military review in
Rome which marked his surrender. They occupy four chapters and part of a fifth. Two chapters only are devoted to
Ostorius' first three years in Britain. If, then, Caratacus
seems to emerge suddenly from the mists of Wales in the
autumn of the year 47, the impression is due to the accident
which deprived us of the earlier part of Tacitus' narrative.

Conjecture is the sole source, and a bold and ingenious
conjecture has recently been made to identify one phase of
Caratacus' operations before he crossed the Severn into
Wales.[2] North of Nailsworth and Minchinhampton, a tongue
of the Cotswolds thrusts boldly towards the Stroud valley,
forming a peninsula of hilly land two miles long and one
mile across, and rising to 700 feet. This naturally strong
defensive position contains Amberley Camp, a hill fort of
the Iron Age 'C' type, and its neck is cut off by The Bul-
warks, a running earthwork resembling the Belgic dykes of
the Colchester region. Here, it has been suggested, was the
stronghold of Caratacus, from which he launched his attacks
on the territory of the allies of Rome – especially on the lands
of those of the Dobunni who had come to terms. Yet, if
archaeological affinities point one way, military probability
surely points the other. It can hardly be supposed that Aulus
Plautius would leave the defiant Belgic king at large so
close – barely a dozen miles – to the Roman *limes*, and free
to range at will into territory so recently subdued. Equally,
Caratacus must have been concerned to place himself beyond the reach of Rome while he mustered forces and supplies to renew the struggle. For both purposes, a link with
the Brigantes was crucial. Wales, and not necessarily South
Wales, is the logical choice.

By AD 47, when he comes once more into focus in the
pages of Tacitus, Caratacus had clearly become the chosen
war-leader of a confederacy of peoples hostile to Rome.
Such a position, implying a supra-tribal military authority,
was held by many great princes of the Celtic world – Cassivellaunus against Caesar in Britain, Vercingetorix, on a
much greater scale, in Gaul. Such, later, was the position of
Boudicca in the rebellion of AD 60. Approved by the chieftains of each of the tribes concerned, the war-leader wielded
powers that were superior but neither absolute nor unques-
tioned. Skill in diplomacy and success in battle were needed
to maintain them. Since the Druids, from their headquarters
in Mona, were steadfast in hostility to Rome, we have deduced that their influence in the choice of Caratacus is
highly probable. How far his direct military authority extended is not clear. Tacitus makes it plain that it was recognized by the Silures, Ordovices and Deceangli; of the attitude of the Demetae we know nothing, but it is hardly likely
that they, alone of the tribes in Wales, could have been
against him. Geographically, a key position was occupied by
the Cornovii, in the gap between the hills of north-east
Wales and the Peak. Whether that tribe was a coherent
political entity at this period is uncertain, but at least some
of them would seem to have supported Caratacus, to judge
from reactions on the Roman side. In short, it would appear
that Caratacus was in control of an area almost identical
with that claimed for himself by Owen Glyndwr in the
Tripartite Indenture of 1403.[3] Diplomatically, his influence
will have extended further. The unsettled tribal politics of
the Brigantes were troubled waters to fish; there was also
discontent among the Iceni. In the old Belgic kingdom
many hopes must have turned to Caratacus, especially from
those who felt the rough edge of Roman rule. Indeed, he
must have been a rallying point for all those elements in the
province who, in Tacitus' words, 'spurned the Roman
peace'.

The account of Tacitus suggests that Caratacus had estab-

lished this position of military and diplomatic strength by
AD 47. A state of hostility already exists. The change of
governors provides the opportunity for a concerted attack
on the territory of friendly tribes, under a central direction
which must surely be his. The invaders are joined by tribes
within the province itself : discontent is so widespread that
the Roman Governor decides to disarm the tribes as soon as
he is able to do so. The problem is to identify the territory
invaded. Tacitus provides no place-names but a clue may be
found in the comment on the methodical strategy of
Ostorius, who 'held fast to his plan, and did not undertake
new enterprises until the ground behind him was firmly consolidated'. As the plan unfolds itself its successive stages are
seen to be : first, the expulsion of the invaders, second, the
disarming of the tribes, and, third, the advance of the Roman
*limes* up to the middle Severn. At this point Ostorius is
diverted to deal with an outbreak of rebellion among the
Iceni, supported by their neighbours. Once the position in
East Anglia is stabilized, his next move is against the Deceangli of Flintshire.[4] The inference seems clear The lands
invaded will certainly include those of the Dobunni, between
the Cotswolds and the Severn, which could be attacked from
Silurian territory. But the Coritani seem also to be affected,
if they were one of the neighbouring tribes which supported
the rebellion of the Iceni, some months later. Cornovian
territory would be the natural base for an assault on them,
and this would account for the Roman decision to bring
under control the 'midland triangle' between Severn and
Trent, a decision which was to add just over one thousand
square miles to the Roman province. Further, that Ostorius
saw as his next step a punitive expedition against the
Deceangli suggests that the epicentre of the whole assault on
the Roman frontier lay on this north-eastern border of
Wales. It is here, then, that we should expect to find Caratacus in the last months of the year 47.

Although Caratacus had made a shrewd choice of the
moment to attack, he underestimated the speed and force of

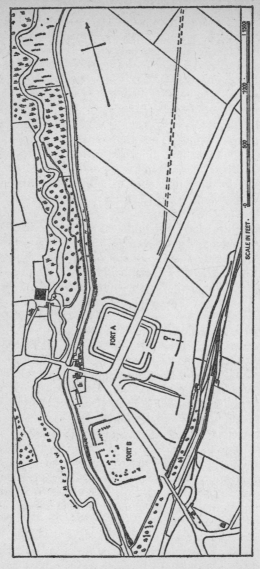

Fig. 5: *The Roman military sites at Greensforge, near Wolverhampton*

the Roman reaction. Ostorius quickly assembled a force of
auxiliary troops for a counter-offensive; the enemy concentrations were dispersed, and invaders chased out of the province. Before the end of 47, the immediate menace was
dispelled. Awkward problems lay ahead. Caratacus himself
would have to be chastened, and further incursions into the
province made impossible. The inadequacy of Aulus Plautius' line of frontier was now evident. It put the Romans too
far east to come to grips with an enemy operating from
Wales. It left far too much of the central midlands in hands
that were hostile, or potentially so. A firm grip on the east
bank of the Severn, from Gloucester to Wroxeter, had become imperative.

But the alarming intransigence of some of the tribes
within the province would also have to be brought under
control. To this end Ostorius decided to disarm all unreliable
elements, a category in which he chose to include the Iceni,
despite their status as a client-kingdom. It was a high-
handed action, and the response was predictable. The Iceni
– or a part of them – turned to war, joined by other rebels
who had perhaps remained under arms since the previous
autumn. East Anglia is not the territory for guerrilla warfare,
but the leaders of the rebellion had provided themselves
with a redoubt – a place, in the words of Tacitus 'protected
by a rude earthwork, and with a narrow approach route, so
as to be impenetrable to cavalry'. Its site has never been
identified. Ostorius himself commanded the Roman force,
which consisted of auxiliary infantry and cavalry: the
legions, it would seem, had been disposed to watch any move
by Caratacus. The cavalry, as such, could not be brought
into operation, but the troopers were dismounted and joined
the infantry in a general assault. The Britons were surrounded and caught in a trap of their own making. They
were overcome after a desperate resistance. These operations
in East Anglia and the midlands will probably have occupied
the summer of AD 48.

II

The archaeological evidence for the activity of Ostorius in
the midland triangle is at present very thin. Only a few sites
have been investigated, and that on a limited scale. Where
work has been done on the military sites in this area it has
become increasingly evident that they have a history complicated by the continual troop movements backwards and
forwards in the decades AD 50–80. Most of them have at least
two if not three permanent forts on the same or nearby sites,
and there are indications of temporary marching camps.

In some cases it seems that the earliest military fort is a
large one, followed by a considerable reduction. This suggests groups of units probing forward in the initial stages,
and smaller holding forces being left behind to consolidate
the gain. A good example of this type of site is at Metchley in
Birmingham, much of it now covered by parts of the Queen
Elizabeth Hospital and the University Medical School.[5] The
larger fort was ten and a half acres and the smaller six and
a quarter acres. Excavation of a corner tower of a four-acre
annex has shown the great timber uprights of the tower
were taken out by driving trenches into the rampart from
the front and the back. Later these open trenches collected
a mass of charcoal representing the burning of the brush-
wood and small timbers. In a recent piece of civic enterprise,
the whole corner tower was rebuilt much as it must have
been originally, but a losing battle was then engaged with
the local youth who found this a heaven-sent target for
destructive games, and no amount of fencing and barbed
wire could keep them out. The whole site has now been
swallowed up by further hospital development, but recent
investigations inside the earlier and larger fort have shown
traces of timber buildings in its southern half. What is
interesting is that the army felt insecure enough to dig in
very thoroughly and erect elaborate corner towers in the
annex. This suggests that Caratacus was falling back slowly

to the Severn behind a screen of skirmishes or that his guer-rilla bands were still very active.

A further eleven miles to the north-west from Metchley brings us to Greensforge where an earthwork was known for a long time as 'Wolverhampton Old Churchyard', a local attempt to explain its origin. A trench was cut across this in 1928 by a party of boys from Wolverhampton Grammar School and a useful section, with the pottery, was published in a manner admirable for its day.[6] Since then aerial photo-graphs have shown that this fort was preceded by a larger marching camp, and another fort about the same size lies in the next field;[7] there are also traces of ditches and other features between the two forts. The photograph of the new fort even shows the post-holes of a gate and corner tower, and also a row of large pits behind the rampart which may be associated with its demolition. Some excavation has been carried out on Fort B (see page 110) by the Kidderminster Society and fourteen coins of Claudius found. But the rela-tionship between the two forts remains uncertain. Much work is needed before the problems of these sites can be solved and the forts and camps fitted into the historical framework. There are similar complications at the little village of Wall, near Lichfield. Here a small but devoted band of amateurs has been excavating almost continuously over the last twelve years, revealing more and yet more problems. The site is on Watling Street, one of the main lines of the Roman advance, and the district has long been known for the remains of Roman buildings. These belonged to the civil town of Leto-cetum; two of its principal buildings, the bath-house and probable *mansio* or hostelry, were found in 1912.[8] The former was studied in more detail in 1956.[9] The little town seems to occupy an area of five to ten acres, but so far its limits have not been defined. Nor is there any trace of the defences which are usually such a marked feature of these settlements. Three parallel ditches have been observed from the air by Dr St Joseph,[10] but they turn out to belong to a small walled enclosure[11] of the fourth century straddling the

Roman road, and excavations have produced no evidence of any substantial building inside; exactly what the function of this defensive work was – either in military or civil terms – it is difficult to understand. It was during the investigation of these late defences that remains were found of the earlier military phases. The few pieces of equipment now in the Department of the Environment site museum include two inscribed tags bearing the punched names of centurions, probably legionaries, so military occupation was not unexpected. A sequence of three or four auxiliary forts appears to have occupied the hill-top position, with pottery down to c AD 75.[12] The earliest military occupation, however, is quite different in character, consisting of timber buildings which spread out to the south of the later forts and of Watling Street itself. No traces of any defences of this fort have been encountered, and its area could extend to the north, east and south for a considerable distance – only to the west does the ground drop away sharply. The pottery associated with these structures fits into the period c AD 45–60. The total of Claudian and pre-Claudian coins found to date including those from the small-scale excavations carried out by the Lichfield and South Staffs Society under Mr A. Round amount to forty-two. In view of the recent work at Wroxeter it would not be too improbable that we have here encountered the fortress of the XIVth Legion, moved into the forward area by Ostorius Scapula. Obviously a great deal more work is needed before this can be argued with conviction; there may be other surprises round the corner.

Proceeding west along Watling Street the next Roman site is the settlement at Pennocrucium. Apart from the civil site there are four different sites at Stretton Mill and Kinvaston, all discovered by Dr St Joseph. The first of these, on a small gravel plateau,[13] looks like a normal auxiliary fort of three-and-a-half acres; a more recent photograph taken by Mr Arnold Baker shows that it was preceded by a larger fort, as at Metchley. The fort at Kinvaston is much larger at twenty-six acres, enough for half a legion. The pottery, found by

Dr St Joseph and in a later excavation,[14] fits into a context
c AD 60 -70 rather than anything earlier, which must imply
that this fort has nothing to do with the Scapulan advance,
but rather with the troop movements during the great revolt of Boudicca in AD 60.[15] However, there are further complications. Dr St Joseph now has evidence that this fort was
also later reduced, this time to eighteen acres, presumably
because troops were needed elsewhere. Yet another site has
been found to the south and east of the others;[16] but no
excavations have yet been carried out. Farther to the west
just to the south of Watling Street, Dr St Joseph has noticed
two marching camps on the same site at Burlington which
must represent a staging point in an advance in this direction.[17] The next site along Watling Street is at Red Hill, a
height which overlooks the Shropshire plain, and here again,
straddling the road, is a small enclosure which must mark the
site of the settlement known as Uxacona. On the higher
ground is a sequence of military sites, but the ditch
systems are somewhat abnormal; they have not yet been
investigated and part of the site is now unfortunately occupied by a reservoir.

On the north-west side of that dominating hog-back the
Wrekin, and by the side of the Severn, stood Viroconium,
capital of the Cornovii, one of the largest and most important towns of Roman Britain. The evidence for its military
origin consists of a series of tombstones of the following soldiers from a nearby cemetery :[18]

1. Tiberius Claudius Tir[.]ntius, a trooper of a Thracian
   cohort
2. Titus Flaminius, a soldier of the XIVth Legion
3. M. Petronius, a standard-bearer of the XIVth Legion
4. Valerius, a soldier probably of the XIVth Legion
5. Caius Mannius Secundus, of the XXth Legion

The presence of at least three stones of soldiers of the XIVth
*Gemina* clearly indicates that it was stationed at or near

Wroxeter, but the memorial of the man of the XXth does not at all imply that this legion was here, as some have thought. This legionary is an old soldier on the Governor's staff, and although he was on the strength of the legion for pay and equipment, he would normally be serving away from it on the business of the Governor (see Appendix IV).

Wroxeter, like the other sites, is beginning to produce complications. To date there are two small forts, three legionary fortresses and two possible marching camps. The first sign of military occupation was noticed by Dr St Joseph – a fort of five acres, 400 yards south of the town on the east bank of the Severn.[19] This fort shows slight abnormalities in the ditch system which may reflect more than one period with probably an earlier marching camp, but the pottery found by Dr St Joseph in a trench and sherds picked up on the surface are Claudian in date, although there is also some later material. This may be the permanent auxiliary fort established by Ostorius Scapula after the advance to the Severn, and the unit could have been the Thracian cohort recorded on the tombstone of Tirentius. Unfortunately the edge of that stone is damaged at the place where the number of the cohort would be given, but it may have been the VIth cohort, originally at Gloucester, which could have moved to these new quarters when the XXth Legion was established there. Another fort was found by Mr Arnold Baker in 1963, a mile north of the Roman city, on the Tern at Duncot. This is an unusually long and narrow shape, 230 feet by 820 feet, as if two auxiliary units had been placed side by side. The siting of this fort is on the main east–west line of advance, whereas the Roman city and the other fort are on the road leading towards the south-west and the Church Stretton gap. It almost seems as if the Duncot fort belongs to an early stage in the drive to the west, and this is confirmed by the presence of two marching camps nearby, one of which is on the disused Atcham airfield. A trench attempting to define the ditch of the latter ran into a deep gun-pit of the last war, an archaeological overlap which gives a gap in time of almost exactly 1,900 years. Neither site has yet produced any datable pottery; if the occupation was short, such evidence may be difficult to find. More recently Mr Arnold Baker has recorded a large fort (about twenty-five acres) and military camps at Eaton Constantine, three miles south-east of Wroxeter, almost under the shadow of the Wrekin.[20] None of these has yet been dated, but the position of the site seems to indicate that it probably belongs to the initial advance and may be connected with the reduction of the Wrekin itself.

Next we must consider the legionary fortresses, which have for some years been a problem that is only now being resolved. The Roman city lies on a sand and gravel plateau and much of its area produces very fine crop-marks of streets and buildings. There has in consequence been a good deal of aerial reconnaissance, specially directed towards finding military sites. It seems odd that after all this search no trace of a fifty-to-sixty-acre fortress has been found. Excavations in the city have produced a quantity of military equipment and Claudian coins, which seems to indicate that the fortress cannot be far away. In 1955 Dr St Joseph recorded two ditches, running under town buildings in the north-west sector and turning a well formed corner,[21] and drew attention to their military character. But this ditch system was on alignment with the town street grid and Professor Sheppard Frere had already demonstrated something of the complexities of early town defences at Verulamium.[22] Caution seemed to be needed before arriving at conclusions. During the course of a training school which was conducted in 1958, a trench was cut across these ditches; but a spell of bad weather and a series of large rubbish pits of later date which had cut into the ditches prevented a section from being completed and studied in detail. It was clear, however, that the ditches were early in the history of the site and there were traces of a timber revetment on the inner lip. All this was hopeful but not conclusive. Meanwhile training schools had continued year by year from 1955 on the site

of the baths; this was slow work, not planned as archaeological investigation, but as training for students in excavating technique. In the areas outside the massive stone
structures of the bath-house whose foundations and base-
ments had removed all the earlier levels, it soon became evident that there were timber buildings of the first century.
These showed as trenches cut into the sand and back-filled
with clean material. They were in fact the type of palisade
trench used by the army to take the upright timbers on
which the buildings were framed. But this was not immediately obvious, and there was the difficulty that these timber foundation works appeared eight feet below present
ground level. If it had been possible to strip a large area to
this depth the full significance of these early buildings would
have been apparent sooner, but the method of working at
that time in square boxes was initiated for training students
rather than solving archaeological problems; it was therefore
some years before a large enough area had been excavated
to demonstrate the nature of these buildings. The situation
was much clarified with the introduction of the open method
of excavation. Gradually it became evident that these buildings were very large, with complex internal arrangements,
and were very different from the simple type of strip-house
usual in early civil development in Roman Britain. Furthermore, there seemed to be at least three periods; in the final
stage the whole had been demolished and the site levelled
out prior to the erection of the first stone buildings on the
site.[23] The historical implications of this need not concern
us here since the pottery, of which there is now a fair quantity, is not earlier than *c* AD 55–60. In other words, if, as
now seems likely, we are in contact with the fortress of the
XIVth Legion, it is evident that it was not established at
Viroconium until that date. The only forts which should
therefore concern us in the period of the initial advance are
the auxiliary ones. Meanwhile, it seems as if the site of the
fortress of the XIVth between *c* AD 50 and 60 must be sought
elsewhere. The evidence of pottery, as suggested above, in-

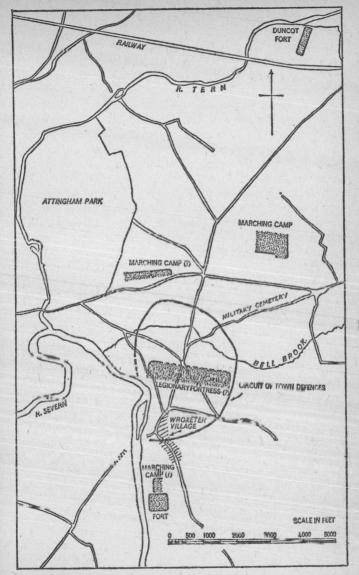

Fig. 6: *The Roman military sites at Wroxeter (Viroconium), Shropshire*

clines one at present towards Wall, undoubtedly a key site in these early years of the conquest.

The Severn must have been a major consideration in the strategy of the Ostorian campaign, but as yet very little evidence has been found of forts along its bank, apart from Gloucester and Wroxeter. Worcester is an obvious site with its Iron Age fort protecting the river crossing.[24] There was a Roman civil settlement here, whose name does not survive, and also of course an important Saxon, medieval and modern city. Unfortunately, the military site probably lies below the Cathedral precinct and the King's School which now stand on the site of the Norman castle. There is also evidence of a fort at Dodderhill near Droitwich, on the high ground overlooking the modern town. Small-scale excavations have produced Claudian pottery[25] and evidence of two periods of occupation, the second of which seems to be in the second century.[26] In the difficult country to the north, including the Ironbridge gap where there must surely be forts, there is so far nothing to report. The later fort near Cleobury Mortimer suggests a crossing of the Severn near Bewdley.

One of the most serious gaps at present is in the evidence of Roman military activity of this period beyond the Severn. It has been too readily assumed in the past that the Roman occupation of the principality started in AD 75 with the governorship of Julius Frontinus. Yet, apart from the deep penetration that Scapula must have made in his campaigns, Tacitus says explicitly that he actually built forts in Silurian territory and was engaged in a bitter guerrilla warfare with the tribe at the time of his death. The only sites which have produced any Claudian material west of the Severn are Usk[27] and Abergavenny[28] where in both cases there is now sufficient from early finds and excavations to postulate forts of this period. These could hardly have existed in splendid isolation; there must be other sites awaiting discovery. There is a remarkable twenty-six acre fort at Clyro near Hay on the Wye, occupying a key position for operations in this valley.

The situation here, as in many of the midland forts, seems to be highly complicated, and only large-scale excavation will produce the full story. The siting and substantial defences of Clyro certainly make it a more permanent fort than has been previously suggested but no satisfactory dating evidence has yet been obtained.[29]

Looking ahead, it is clear that the failure of Ostorius Scapula to bring the Silures to heel after the defeat of Caratacus made it necessary for him to maintain considerable forces in their territory; for to have retreated to the Severn and established his frontier on the east bank might have looked like defeat. The Roman Army seems thus to have been committed to maintaining a frontier in most difficult circumstances against an actively hostile population in hilly, forested terrain.

As the evidence accumulates year by year from casual finds, aerial reconnaissance and emergency excavations proceeding from development and motorways, it is becoming clear that the limit of the territory held under Scapula at the southern end was the River Usk. Possible sites at Usk and Abergavenny have already been postulated above. The mouth of the river and its estuary would need protection and a fort should be sought under or near Newport. There is a small two-and-a-half-acre fort at Coed-y-Caerau in a very commanding position, but not yet dated.[30] The difficulties start when one tries to project the line to the north towards the Wye. One possibility is the Monnow Valley where a Roman road is known, reaching the Wye at Kenchester, where harness[31] pendants signify the possible presence of a cavalry unit; this would place Clyro in a forward position. Thence to the north the line seems clear from the great Roman road which sweeps over the Hereford Plain towards the Church Stretton gap, but so far the only site is one of the Leintwardine complex at Jay Lane. The evidence from the excavations of Mr S. C. Stanford is far from conclusive, but a good case is made for pre-Flavian occupation.[32] Dr St Joseph has a site pieced together from a number of sorties at Wistanstow, north of Craven Arms, but as yet undated.[33] Between this line and the River Severn a number of forts are to be expected, but the only hints are at :

(1) Ariconium, the main iron-smelting settlement of later times where some early coins may be indicative.[34]
(2) Stretton Grandison where Arnold Baker has a fort of almost five acres.[35]
(3) Wall Town near Cleobury Mortimer where a Flavian fort has been investigated,[36] and there may be an earlier one nearby.

### III

The advance to the middle Severn brought much of the territory of the Cornovii under Roman control, and from bases on this new frontier it would be easy to strike at any of their malcontents still in arms. But the problems of the Deceangli remained, and the Roman commander must have been anxious to explore the territory between the Welsh hills and the south-western approaches to Brigantia, where military action might soon be needed. Perhaps he had in mind a Roman base in this area, to correspond to Lincoln in the east. The campaigning season of AD 49 was devoted to these objectives. Only one geographical detail is given for the attack on the Deceangli in this, the first Roman penetration into Wales. The concise account of Tacitus reads like many of the Welsh wars of English kings in the early Middle Ages. 'Their lands were ravaged, and booty was collected on all sides. The natives did not venture on a pitched battle, and when they did try to harass the column from ambush, their treachery was punished.' The Deceangli, it is clear, used sensible guerrilla tactics, whether at the instance of Caratacus or of their own leaders. The mention of lands laid waste gives some clue to the route taken by the Roman army, for the distribution of hill-forts makes it clear that some of the best lands of the Deceangli were in the Vale of Clwyd. How did the Romans reach them? The modern traveller approaching from the south-east enjoys the beautiful Vale of Llangollen and the spectacular road over the Horseshoe Pass; but this would be a dangerous approach for an invading army venturing into unknown territory. A more promising line would be up the valley of the River Alyn past Mold, then by Bodfari and the River Wheeler to the neighbourhood of Denbigh. A little farther north, too, lies the route followed by the later Roman road, from Pentre Halkyn to the crossing of the Clwyd at St Asaph.

But Ostorius' problems were not confined to the Deceangli. 'They had almost reached the sea which looks towards Ireland, when trouble broke out among the Brigantes and forced the Roman general to retrace his steps . . .' The point of return, perhaps, was somewhere near St Asaph or Rhuddlan. Intervention in Brigantia was now required. Here we may suspect the influence of Caratacus in the warparty of that nation, who became alarmed at the possibility of being outflanked, and cut off from Wales. 'The few who took up arms were killed, the rest were pardoned' : again, Tacitus does not help to place events on the map. But the Romans presumably went as far as the upper Mersey, and one notes the hill-forts (Mam Tor, etc) on the western slopes of the Peak. The northern Camulodunum (Almondbury, near Huddersfield) was an important political centre : it is just possible that the Roman Army penetrated so far in support of Queen Cartimandua. Certainly Tacitus here implies both military action and a political settlement. By the time these were concluded, the season for campaigning was over and the Roman units were withdrawn to base.

It would be quite possible for Ostorius to present the year's work in a favourable light, and his attempt to do so seems to have been the source for Tacitus. Yet his objectives (if we have defined them correctly) were largely unattained. He had now learned something of the topography of north-east Wales, and of the problems of coming to closer grips with the Brigantes. But the Roman frontier remained as it

had been, and the fighting strength of the Deceangli was un-
impaired and able to stand again with Caratacus another
year.

IV

At this point a reappraisal must have been forced on the
Roman Governor. After two years of office, the problems
ahead of him were far more formidable than any he had yet
solved. The policy of dealing with the tribes individually, ap-
plying *clementia* or *atrocitas* as the case demanded, had
failed: thanks to Caratacus, there was a cohesion among them
for which he had not allowed. Above all, there was the hostility of the Silures. The most warlike and the most powerful of
the Welsh tribes, neither diplomacy nor force had as yet the
slightest effect on them. Operations must already have been
undertaken in the difficult country between the Severn and
the Wye, and would have shown that it was impossible to
control them from the auxiliary forts established by Aulus
Plautius along the lower Severn. A major campaign must
now be undertaken in South Wales, and the main strength
of the legions be brought to bear on the Silures. More was
involved in this deployment than a simple march to the
west. Discontent was still alive in the eastern part of the province, and it would not do to leave it stripped of forces.

Against this background, Ostorius' decision to found a
military colony at Camulodunum is seen as the logical appli-
cation of a well-tried policy. It had been a legionary base
since AD 43. The legions had now been in Britain for six
years, and it may be assumed that – had there been no dis-
charges – between a quarter and a third of the men were
now due for retirement. Their land-grants could come from
the estates of the royal house of Cunobelinus: Camulodunum was famous throughout the island, and easily reached
from the Continent. Here, too, the eleven British kings had
surrendered to Claudius in AD 43. No other place seemed
so suitable for the capital of the province, the centre of the

cult of Claudius, and the show-piece of civilization. The strong force of veterans (perhaps two or three thousand men?), established here by Ostorius on a new site close to the old native capital in the winter of 49–50, had a double purpose to discharge. A reserve to be used in case of trouble, they were also expected, with the example of their unswerving loyalty to Rome, 'to instruct the friendly natives in the duties enjoined by the laws'. In view of the history of the colony, Tacitus' words have an ironic ring. For the overbearing arrogance and greed of the veterans of Camulodunum did more than anything else to induce the Trinovantes to join the tribal cause under Boudicca only eleven years later (AD 60). Not much can be said for the veterans of Camulodunum. But perhaps it should be remembered that these same men, six years earlier, had regarded an expedition to Britain as taking them beyond the limits of the known world. It cannot have pleased them to know that they were now expected to live there for the rest of their lives. But Ostorius could hardly have appreciated the full consequences of his decision. His needs were immediate and urgent. There were two main objectives – to replace the older troops and to transfer his only available legion, the XXth, to its new base at Gloucester, the springboard for the thrust into South Wales.

Various attempts to find the fortress in the Kingsholm area were unsuccessful until 1972, when a small area was excavated in advance of long-term development by Mr Henry Hodges of the Gloucester Museum. He found a timber building associated with Claudian pottery and military equipment. This building had not been totally dismantled, as is customary when the army leaves a site, but reduced so that the lower few feet of walling survived; at least all that actually remained were the plaster faces, painted in panels. The wood itself had decayed and the space between the plaster filled with earth, falling in from above as the timbers rotted. In the first season's work only a small part of this building could be explored and its military character not proved. The

most significant finds were, however, pits dug into the building containing large fragments of Neronian pottery.[37] This is
what could be expected on the departure of the legion in 67
to go to Wroxeter.[38] This then was a military area if not a
building abandoned at this time and is strong evidence of a
military presence for the period *c* 50–67.

V

The winter of 49–50 must have been a busy one for Ostorius,
with the affairs of the *colonia* to supervise, as well as all the
preparations for the most serious campaigns in Britain since
the invasion itself. At last all was ready. *Itum inde in Siluras.*
Early in the summer of AD 50, the XXth Legion, in the full
panoply of a Roman army marching out for battle, left its
base at Gloucester to cross the Severn and advance towards
the hills of South Wales. Yet another force may have left
Viroconium, to probe up the Severn valley towards Caersws,
and to stop reinforcements reaching Caratacus from the
north. A fort and three marching camps have been observed
by Dr St Joseph at Brompton about four miles south-east of
the later permanent fort at Forden Gaer. But Ostorius was
not to lay his foe by the heels that summer. The Roman
forces were operating in difficult country and against a wily
opponent – the first general in history, it would seem, to
view the military problems of Wales as a whole. If actions
were fought, Tacitus does not mention them. Caratacus had
plenty of room to manoeuvre, and it would suit him well to
let the Romans exhaust themselves in long marches while he
was continually threatening an engagement but always
slipping away. Ostorius, too, may have been content simply
to get to know the routes into the mountains and round
their flanks, to explore the river valleys and to select sites for
a network of forts that would ensure a permanent Roman
hold on the country. Doubtless booty was taken wherever
possible and settlements burned to discourage the people
from lending help to the enemy. Marching camps are known

in the Ludlow gap at Bromfield [39] and near Craven Arms,[40] at Brampton Bryan [41] and at the crossing of the Onny near Stretford Bridge,[42] also in Glamorgan on Silurian territory.[43] None of them can be dated, at present, but some may well belong to these operations. Perhaps, too, a column will have advanced down the western bank of the Severn to Chepstow, where a discerning eye could have noted its unsuitability as a supply base because of the great range of the tides. There may have been a fort here at this important crossing but the only hint of it has been the discovery of a harness mount.[44]

Coupled with these probes into the Welsh Marches would have been extensive naval patrols. Operating from the Bristol Channel and the north coast of Devon, the squadron sweeping along the southern Welsh shore must have perturbed the Silures with the prospect of a sea-borne invasion while their main fighting strength was elsewhere.[45] No protection could be offered on the water and the galleys paraded up and down: the precise rhythm of their oars gave the shore watchers cause for alarm. There are two small signal-stations on the coast of Devon, at Old Burrow and Martinhoe. Excavations have shown that the first of these could well belong to this period, with coins of Tiberius and Claudius and a military entrenching tool. Martinhoe has produced coins of Nero (AD 64–8) and either continued in use or belongs to a later occasion.[46]

To gain control of the coastline and the Bristol Channel, the army took over the whole of the Devonian peninsula. Exeter may now have become the main base for this operation.[47] The remarkable discoveries in the Cathedral Green seem to indicate the presence of a large bath-house of the mid-first century. If this is military it must be legionary but one is reluctant to agree with such an important conclusion on quite meagre dating evidence. What is much more certain is the existence of long timber buildings of this period which may be barrack-blocks some distance to the north.[48] There is military activity over a large area but its full sig-

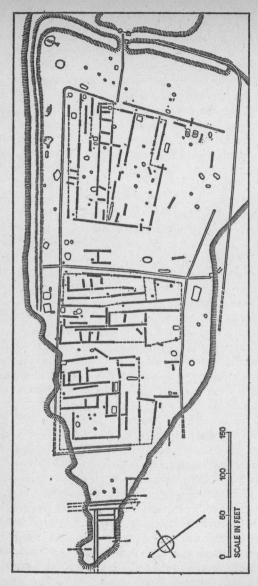

SCALE IN FEET
0    50    100    150

Fig. 7: Plan of the Claudian fort at Waddon Hill, Dorset

nificance cannot be fully understood without more work, particularly on the defences of a fort, fortress or a sequence of defended sites. There is a Roman road from Exeter and the first site on it, sixteen miles away, is the six-and-a-half-acre fort near North Tawton, the ramparts of which are still clearly visible on the ground. There should be another at the important crossing of the Tamar, yet to be located. Beyond this, by the River Camel, lies the fort at Tregear Farm, Nanstallon, near Bodmin. Excavations were carried out by Lady Aileen Fox and Professor W. L. D. Ravenhill, from 1965–69. Finds indicate the date range c AD 55–80 and the plan of the eastern half of the 2.2-acre fort has been established. This included the central building, the *principia* and the adjacent *praetorium* (commandant's house) and four barrack blocks. Unfortunately, the finds of metalwork are not helpful in the identification of the unit. The fact that one of the barrack blocks is larger than the other does suggest both cavalry and infantry with the possibility that the fort housed part of a *cohors equitata*. A coin of Nero of AD 64–66 was found in the construction trench of one of the barracks and shows that, while the fort was probably established by Scapula as a fortified camp, it was being organized at a later date into a permanent fort. Nor must one overlook the importance of Sea Mills as the main ferry route across the Bristol Channel, and it is unfortunate that so little is known about the site, now lost to development (see p. 86 above).

The forward movement was accompanied by withdrawals in the rear. The Romans could no longer afford to have their units spread over the south-east regions. The need for more first-line troops on the frontier, seen in the transfer of the XXth to the lower Severn, is symptomatic of this forward movement. Forts at places like Verulamium and Silchester must have been abandoned at this stage. Occupation ceased also at Hod Hill while new forts came into being to the west. One of these was at Waddon Hill, near Beaminster, Dorset, also on a hill-top but which had not been previously occupied. Unfortunately, half the hill had been removed by stone quarrying which only ceased in this century. During this period many objects and coins were found, some being acquired by Ralls, a Bridport corn-merchant, eventually to find their way into the Bridport Museum where they lay in a dark corner for many years, their significance unnoticed. The most interesting of these items is undoubtedly the fine dagger-scabbard first seen as a mass of rust, but recognized by its shape. After careful cleaning an inlaid pattern of gold-alloy emerged, but much of the detail had been lost. Excavations carried out from 1959–1969 have revealed the plans of several buildings (see p. 128) but they do not have the completed appearance of those at Hod Hill.[49] The most westerly building was probably the *principia*, headquarters, and all that has been preserved is at the rear of the fort. The elongated shape is due entirely to the configuration of the hilltop and its steep sides to the north and south.

The work at Waddon has produced a few details which help to throw a light on the life of the soldiers. For example, the bulk of the pottery used for cooking and eating was obtained from native potters. It consisted of typical Durotrigian bowls and jars in a black, highly burnished ware. But the troops also needed other vessels such as mixing bowls (*mortaria*) and flagons – forms new to Britain. These were either imported or else local potters were quick to imitate Romanized types. A kiln of this period was found at Corfe Mullen not far from the base at Hamworthy mentioned above. The products were mostly *mortaria* and flagons, but native-type jars and bowls were also made here. This shows that Corfe Mullen could hardly have been a works-depot but rather the kiln of a Durotrigian potter successfully producing the kind of wares needed for this new market. Whether he operated under contract or duress it would be difficult to show. Rubbish pits inside the fort gave some indication of military diet – apart from the usual animal bones there were also those of fish, notably the Giant Wrasse, a very bony fish which modern anglers throw back into the sea. Of the 101 bones of hare, 81 are parts of the foot, probably used as lucky charms. There is a large number of small black and white glass counters, relics of gambling or they may have been used for counting, as jettons were used in the Middle Ages.

Little military glory was won by the Roman Army that summer, but at the end of it Ostorius probably felt that he had learned enough about the country of the Silures to turn it into a trap for Caratacus. Another season the trap could be sprung.

Caratacus, who will have made his own appraisal, seems to have reached the same conclusion. Ostensibly, he had done well to keep Roman power at bay for a further year, but the performance could hardly be repeated. Perhaps, too, there were growing tensions in his relations with the tribes of Wales, at which we can only guess. His policy meant virtually the maintenance of a standing army, something alien to the Celtic traditions of warfare. There were compensations so long as booty could be had by raiding the Roman province, but the new frontier defences of Ostorius ruled that out. The economic burden of maintaining Caratacus' own force must have been considerable. Henceforward, there was the prospect of a war each summer on Welsh soil – and the Deceangli and the Silures could testify what that would mean. *Atrocitas* was beginning to pay dividends. The position of a war-leader in a confederacy of Celtic peoples was precarious : success was an essential ingredient. There could have been many grumbles against Caratacus that winter among the tribal chieftains of Wales. Considerations such as these forced the British general to seize the initiative for the campaign of AD 51, and to fight on new ground and with a new strategy. In Tacitus' account,[50] there is a justifiable note of surprise : 'Next Caratacus, inferior to us in numbers, but superior in cunning and knowledge of the country, transferred the fighting to the country of the Ordovices. Joined by all who feared the '*pax Romana*', he determined to stake everything on a pitched battle. He had chosen a site where the approach routes, lines of retreat, and all other factors were to his advantage and our disadvantage . . .'

Before discussing the vexed question of where this place of strength may be, it is necessary to try to understand the hopes on which Caratacus' new policy was based. The move to the land of the Ordovices, from south-east to central and northern Wales, is obvious enough. It avoids encirclement on the Black Mountains by a Roman thrust up the Wye and the Usk. It keeps open the lines of communication with Brigantia, for reinforcements as well as for retreat – hence the presence of those who 'feared the Roman peace'. But the decision to choose a strong place to stand and fight is different : it is not thus that inferior forces can usually hope to win a Welsh campaign. Caratacus must have foreseen no future for himself in Wales unless he could win a decisive victory. And history afforded grounds for such hope – the same grounds that had prompted resistance to the invasion of AD 43. If a strong enough position could be found, the Romans might be led on to disaster, and then there would be a free Wales at least. And if he lost, the struggle could be renewed in Brigantia. So once more the tribal levies gathered round Caratacus and the Belgic war-band he had brought to Wales. We do not know how numerous were the dissidents who rallied to him from Brigantia and from within the province, but he must have headed a formidable body of fighting men, hating the Roman invader and convinced that their cause was just.

In the fighting of 51, Ostorius had to play a hand where the cards had been dealt by Caratacus. How long it took him to discover the chosen redoubt, whether there was any preliminary skirmishing, whether he waited for his forces to unite or used the northern column alone for the final battle, we do not know. Tacitus, with his instinct for the dramatic, hurries on to describe the Roman forces halted in front of a river whose fords are unknown. Beyond it the hills rise steeply, their slopes bristling with armed men. So we reach that famous site which, as Haverfield complains, 'the imagination of local antiquaries has placed on every hill-top in the Border'. Such imaginations were too seldom controlled by a close study of the words of Tacitus : 'a site where the approach routes, lines of retreat, and all other factors were to his advantage and our disadvantage. On the one side were steep hills, and where they did offer an easier line of ascent they had piled boulders to form a rampart. A river flowed in front of the position, and its fords had not been tested, while bands of armed warriors lined the defences.' Further, the account of the battle makes it clear that the steep slopes rose to a summit plateau, while the escape of Caratacus suggests a place not easily surrounded, and with good lines of escape to the north and north-east. To summarize – a complex group of hills, rising above a large river, with a summit plateau, in the land of the Ordovices – these are the conditions which any candidate for the position is required to satisfy. Reflection will suggest other negative indications. It is not a hill-fort of the ordinary kind – the defences have had to be improvised. It is hardly likely to be in the mountains of Snowdonia – Caratacus will not go so far north-west lest he be cornered and cut off from Brigantia Nor is it anywhere in north-east Wales, for that is the land of the Deceangli. Somewhere then, in north-central Wales : and if so, there would seem to be only two suitable rivers, the upper Severn and the Dee. No site along the Dee impresses us, but there are two on the Severn whose claims we rank high.

The first of these, Cefncarnedd, has a long-standing local tradition, now revived by the distinguished support of Dr J. K. St Joseph.[51] It forms part of a line of hills between Caersws and Llanidloes, rising on a front of rather more than four miles to the west of the Severn, with the valley of the Tarann and its tributaries on the opposite side. Cefncarnedd (908 feet) itself is the northernmost point of the group which reaches a height of 1,007 feet at Gelli Hir. Dr St Joseph rightly draws attention to the strategic importance of this site at the junction of routes to South Wales, the Shropshire plain, and Cardigan Bay. The succession of Roman forts at Caersws, and the railway junction at Moat Lane, were founded to take advantage of this nodal point of communications in Wales.[52] He points out how admirably this great natural amphitheatre would serve as the focus of the southernmost sept of the Ordovices. It would, indeed, and such no doubt was the function of the hill-fort which has given its name to Cefncarnedd. But a close inspection shows these hills at a disadvantage as the site of Caratacus' redoubt. As seen from Llandinam, Cefncarnedd does not rise very steeply above the river, and there is flat land on either side which could contain large Roman forces before and after the crossings. Moreover, Cefncarnedd itself is cut off from the rest of the group by an easy pass, now followed by the minor road from Llandinam to Trewythen. Further south, the Wigdwr Brook gives another easy line of penetration. The position, in fact, could be easily surrounded and the cavalry patrols would be lax indeed to allow Caratacus to escape.

We would therefore draw attention to another site some three miles to the east of Newtown, just opposite Abermule. Here, on a front of rather more than a mile, between Dolforwyn Hall and Aberbechan, the hills rise very steeply from the north bank of the Severn to about 800 feet. The strategic importance of this site is marked by Dolforwyn Castle : it must be conceded there is no sign or tradition whatsoever of any Roman or pre-Roman antiquities. But – and this is the point – once the plateau by Dolforwyn Castle is gained, a tangled mass of hilly country, nowhere much above 1,000 feet but deeply dissected by streams, is seen stretching northwards for some ten miles to the valley of the Vyrnwy to the east of Llanfair Caereinion. Such country could not be easily patrolled, and, once the Vyrnwy is reached, the broad Vale of Meifod leads north-east to the Shropshire plain, the Dee and the Mersey. We present these two places on a short-list, without venturing a final choice. Archaeology may one day decide between them, or produce a better candidate.

VI

For the battle that followed, Tacitus is the only guide. His description [53] is one of the best of the four surviving British battle scenes, and is marked by the speed and concinnity of his mature powers. Such literary set-pieces are specially designed for the reader's pleasure : it may be that some of their flavour will survive translation.

The British chieftains went round their tribal levies, making light of their fears, encouraging their hopes, and offering other incentives to arms. Caratacus hastened from one point to the next, proclaiming that this was the day and this the battle which would either win back their freedom, or mark the beginning of eternal slavery. He called on the names of their ancestors, who had put to flight the dictator Julius Caesar; it was through their valour that they lived free from the lictor's axe and the tax-collector's demands, and that the bodies of their wives and children were undefiled. These words were greeted with applause, and every man bound himself, with the oath of his people, never to yield to weapons or wounds. Their spirit dismayed the Roman commander, as did the river between the armies, the strengthened defences, the overhanging ridges, and the fierce warriors who crowded every point. All made up a black picture. But the soldiers demanded battle, saying that valour could carry any position : their officers spoke in the same way and encouraged them still further. Then Ostorius made a reconnaissance to determine which points would yield and which would not, and led forward his eager troops. The river-crossing offered no obstacle. When they reached the embankment, there was a sharp exchange of missiles, with more deaths and casualties on the Roman side. But then they locked shields to form a 'tortoise', hurled down the rudely-built rampart, and brought about a hand-to-hand battle on equal terms. The barbarians retreated to the hill-top, but here too our men followed them, the light-armed auxiliaries using their spears, the legionaries in close order. The British ranks were thrown into confusion, for they had no protection from breast-plate or helmets : if they made a stand against the auxiliaries, they were mown down by the swords and spears of the legionaries, if they turned against the latter, they met the long swords and pikes of the auxiliaries. It was a glorious victory : the wife and daughter of Caratacus were captured, and his brothers surrendered. He himself fled to Cartimandua, Queen of the Brigantes. But there is no refuge in adversity, and he was bound in chains and handed over to us. This was the ninth year of the war in Britain.

The passage is masterly in its selection of significant detail – the nature of the country, the feelings of the contestants, the issues at stake for the Britons, the successive phases of the battle, and the technical superiority by which victory was won. Like the scenes on Trajan's Column – almost contemporary with the *Annals* – it gives the essence of a battle, as recorded by a great artist. So, at Stratford, the words of Shakespeare, the skill of producer and actor, and the dreadful ringing of steel on steel, conveyed the essence of the Wars of the Roses. But questions are now in order, and modern accounts of battles call for more details than these. First, what were the numbers engaged on both sides? The statement that the Roman general had the larger forces refers presumably to the campaign as a whole rather than to this battle. Two legions with auxiliaries would give Ostorius Scapula some 20,000 troops deployed in Wales, of whom perhaps between 12,000 and 15,000 might have taken part in the last battle. The army of Caratacus, then, is not likely to have exceeded 10,000 men. This was a confederate army, made up of tribal contingents. How many, and from which tribes? The description suggests at least three, possibly more. The Silures, Ordovices and Deceangli are certain contributors, perhaps the Demetae, and a rebel force from the Brigantes in addition to Caratacus' own Belgae. In all, some five contingents at least, each fighting under its own leaders. The rebellion of Civilis in Gaul (AD 70) offers parallels on a larger scale. At the siege of Vetera the Batavians and the German tribes were posted 'each tribe by itself, so that in isolation the valour of each could be more clearly seen'. At the same site but in the later battle which was to decide the issue of the rebellion, Civilis was in command of a contingent from the Batavi, the Cugerni, and two or more German tribes.[54] Such heterogeneous barbarian armies must have presented problems of command which Roman generals were spared. A contest of valour might be useful, if the day went well : in adversity each group would be only too likely to look after itself. No wonder that the Britons were called upon to swear, 'each man by the oath of his tribe', to resist to the end. Such tribal oaths, incidentally, are familiar in the battles in the hero-tales of Ireland. And in other respects, too, Tacitus has caught the spirit of a great Celtic host. The fierce appearance of the warriors and their wild costumes, the clash of arms and the raucous blast of the *carnyx*, the Celtic trumpet, the impassioned appeal of the chieftains - all this sound and fury could shake even experienced Roman troops. One senses, too, that an ingredient in the *atrox spectaculum* which disconcerted Ostorius and his men was the day itself. One of those lowering days perhaps, too common in a Welsh summer, when the clouds hang low and black, and the mountains look higher and steeper than they really are. But, as the soldiers said, courage would carry the day. A battle now, they probably felt, would be better than more footslogging round the hills of Wales in the rain.

The engagement itself falls into three clearly defined phases. First, the river-crossing. Once the fords had been found, this proved easier than expected : here it may be said

that there are four fords in little more than a mile in front
of the Dolforwyn position. It does not seem to have been a
contested crossing – though harassed by missiles no doubt –
for the Britons were reserving their main efforts for resistance at the rock-barriers. With cover, and the advantage of
the slope, they were able to inflict sizeable losses at these
points, but the *testudo* formation proved its value once
again. Caratacus, unlike some of the tribes beyond the Rhine
frontier, had not had much practice in the art of fortification. Driven from their defences to the summit-plateau, the
Britons felt in full measure the Roman superiority in
weapons and armour. The short, rigid stabbing sword of the
legionary always had a deadly margin over the long cutting
sword of the Celt : but now, too, the specialized weapons
of the auxiliaries came into play. Only the British chieftains
wore helmets and armour – the common soldiers had to go
into action almost naked – indeed, they may have preferred
it, as Highland troops have sometimes done even in modern
times. In tribal warfare this would not matter, but against
a Roman army they were placed at a fatal disadvantage. It
was at this point that the British ranks gave way, and the
day was lost. So far the battle had followed the classic pattern for engagements between Roman and Celtic forces. But
there was usually a final phase that is here absent – pursuit
and slaughter. No British casualty figures are given for this
battle, in contrast to the 10,000 claimed at Mons Graupius,
or 80,000 for Suetonius' victory over Boudicca.[55] Now pursuit and slaughter is the task of the cavalry, and there is no
mention of Roman cavalry – nor of British chariots – in
Tacitus' account. Clearly the battle was fought over country
where cavalry was useless or could operate only with difficulty – another pointer to Caratacus' skilled choice of
ground. It is worth comparing this battle with the similar
action fought by Petilius Cerialis against the rebellious Treveri under Valentinus.[56] This took place at Rigodulum
(Riol), a strong position in the Moselle Valley between Trier
and Bingen. The hill of Rigodulum is much higher than

either of our sites in the upper Severn, and the Moselle is a
larger river : there, too, the enemy occupied the position in
force, and had built defensive works at weak points. But
Cerialis was able to use his cavalry in the frontal assault on
the hill : more important still, another force worked its way
round over easier ground, and coming from the Hunsruck
took the Treveri in the rear, 'capturing Valentinus and the
Belgic chiefs'. Such a catch did not fall to Ostorius. Caratacus' brothers surrendered, no doubt in the course of the
fighting. His wife and daughter were captured – by what
mischance we do not know. But Caratacus escaped again, as
he did from the battle at the Medway, and it is likely that
horses hidden on the flatter ground of the plateau will have
carried him, with a small force of bodyguard, out of reach of
any Roman pursuit. Others too seem to have got safely
away. Only a few months later the Silures are found fighting
with undaunted ferocity 'to avenge the defeat of so great a
king'. The inference is clear – the action on the Severn made
no heavy inroads on their fighting strength, nor perhaps on
that of the other Welsh tribes. Caratacus will have given the
order to disperse before he made his own escape.

For Ostorius, of course, it was indeed a famous victory,
and it had shattered the British confederacy. But it is clear
that Caratacus did not think it the end of the war. That this
is so follows from the course he now took – escape to Brigantia. Tacitus pictures this as the action of a desperate fugitive
who throws himself on the mercy of Cartimandua, only to
be betrayed by her and delivered up to the Romans. There
are good grounds for mistrusting this assessment. If all Caratacus wanted was a bolt-hole, there were not lacking in
Wales places where he and a few friends could have maintained themselves, even for years, as Owen Glyndwr did after
the battle of Shrewsbury. The Snowdon massif, for example,
where he would have the support of the Ordovices and the
Druids. Or the lonely wilderness of Plynlimmon, or the steep
green mountains and deep cwms of Mawddwy, from which
in the mid-sixteenth century the Gwylliaid Cochion or Red

Banditti terrorized the countryside for years, defying all attempts to round them up. Had he felt, like Commius, King of the Atrebates, that he would go where he would never look on a Roman again, he could have fled to Ireland. That he rejected these possibilities in favour of Brigantia makes his purpose clear – the renewal of the war. The long-term prospects for such a course would have seemed promising. The Brigantes were a powerful and warlike people, and though the anti-Roman party was in eclipse for the moment, with his help it could perhaps gain the ascendancy. If so, the Pennines would be the ideal country for the British resistance : better than Wales, because behind them lay the man-power and fastnesses of Caledonia. The Silures were still in the field, and, if contact with Wales could be kept, it might be possible to concert an attack against the province on two fronts. Caratacus could still offer a threat to Rome. But the immediate hazards were obvious. Chief among them was the position of Cartimandua. He would depend on her sympathy, initially, though no doubt the diplomatic spadework had already been done to renew in the north his powers as war-leader. After all, when he fled to Wales he had been in just this situation.

It is at this point that Queen Cartimandua, whose political and amorous adventures were to play so large a part in the history of Britain for the next eighteen years, is first mentioned by name in the historical narrative of Tacitus, as we have it. Had his account of the Claudian invasion survived, we should know whether – as seems almost certain – she was indeed the ruler of the Brigantes when that state first became a client-kingdom. The heiress of a royal house whose male line was extinct, she sat on an uneasy throne. Geography and politics alike made for centrifugal tendencies among the Brigantes. Links between the royal line and that of Cunobelinus have been suspected, but not proved; archaeology discloses cultural ties with the Druids of Mona and the tribes of north-east Wales and its borders.

Caratacus cannot have come as a stranger to the Queen

of the Brigantes, but his presence must have seemed full of
menace. She ruled over a faction-ridden state with the support of Rome. Without it, perhaps, she would have lost her
throne, as she so nearly did eighteen years later. Her enemies were the enemies of Rome : to shelter Caratacus would
be to help them to power. To what ties of kinship or patriot-
ism or religion Caratacus appealed we do not know. He
spoke to deaf ears. And when a Roman mission appeared to
demand his surrender, it was in the logic of the situation
that she should comply. Caratacus in chains – what greater
service could she render to Rome? For not merely did it
seem to put an end to the war in Britain, but it was most
useful to official propaganda. The prestige of Claudius'
regime had been badly shaken by the excesses of the freedmen and the scandals of Messalina, culminating in her death
in AD 47. The new Empress, Agrippina, was anxious to pro-
mote great State ceremonies at which she could appear as
consort : Claudius himself had a taste for such occasions,
whether from policy or private inclination. The capture of
Caratacus could be made to recall the glorious days of AD 44
– and not only in Rome. Tacitus leaves no doubt that
Caratacus with his family and retinue appeared in a series
of public displays virtually all the way from Britain to the
capital. 'His fame had spread beyond the British islands, had
penetrated the western provinces, and was well-known in
Italy itself. All were eager to see the man who had so long
defied Roman power.' Of the details of this journey we know
nothing and can only imagine its effects on Caratacus' mind.
As he passed through the northern parts of Gaul he would
have seen the growing prosperity of a land that had learned
to accept the Roman rule. Then followed, perhaps, the
splendour of Lugdunum and the cities of Gallia Narbonen-
sis. Did he see the triumphal arch at Arausio (Orange) in
honour of Caesar's victories, and realize that the man
'defeated by my ancestors' had some solid and permanent
achievements to his credit in Celtic lands? All this is conjecture. But that the magnificence and power of Roman

civilization impressed him deeply is clear from what he said in Rome.

The surrender of Caratacus was regarded, so Tacitus says, as an embellishment of the triumph of Claudius. It was also thought (wrongly) to mark the end of the fighting in Wales, and indeed in Britain, for the arrangement with the client kingdom of the Brigantes had held firm under stress. With the surrender of the last of Cunobelinus' sons, Claudius' objectives in Britain could be taken as attained. There could hardly be another triumph, but the occasion was marked by a grand military review and a special session of the Senate.

The review was held on the parade-ground of the Praetorian Guard, with the city cohorts under arms, and the Roman people looking on. Claudius sat on a tribunal with Agrippina at his side; a novelty which drew unfavourable comment from Tacitus, but another sign of the importance accorded to the Empress and to the Imperial House.[57] There was a parade of captives, as in a triumph. 'As the King's followers marched along, their decorations and torcs and the spoils they had won in wars against the other British tribes were displayed. Then came Caratacus' brothers, his wife and daughter, finally the King himself ...' There follows the famous speech of Caratacus :

Had my high birth and rank been accompanied by moderation in the hour of success, I should have entered this city as a friend and not a prisoner. You would not have hesitated to accept as an ally a man of splendid ancestry, bearing rule over many tribes. My present position is degrading to me, but glorious to you. I had horses, warriors, and gold : if I was unwilling to lose them, what wonder in that? Does it follow that, because you desire universal empire, all must accept universal slavery? Were I now dragged here as one who had surrendered without

fighting, no fame would have attached to my fall nor to
your victory. If you punish me they will both be forgotten.
Spare me, then, to be an eternal example of your mercy!

Short as it is, it must rank with the best of Tacitean
speeches. But is it more than a rhetorical composition? Can
it be used by the historian of Roman Britain? Now while
Tacitus does not claim to reproduce the words of a speaker,
he uses speech to throw light on the motives of the speaker
and the facts of the situation. This ceremony was obviously
carefully stage-managed, and needed a speech from Caratacus as its climax. And there is evidence, apart from Tacitus,
to show that he did speak and that what he said was remembered. Zonaras, following Dio Cassius, records his comment
on Roman magnificence. 'And when you have all this, do
you still envy us our hovels?' [58] Granted that we may use
Caratacus' speech in the *Annals* as evidence, there are three
things to be noted. First, a suggestion that he once had the
chance of coming to terms with Rome, but turned it down.
The words, with a suggestion of an offer of client kingship,
fit best into the context of the diplomatic offensive earlier
alluded to (p. 34). The second is his steady belief in the
value of *libertas*, in defiance of all the aims of Roman im-
perialism. And the third – his appeal to the *clementia* or
mercy of the Emperor.

This last is the real point of the speech, and is underlined
by what was said in the 'long and extravagant speeches' in
the special session of the Senate. The surrender of Caratacus
was compared to the display of Syphax by Scipio Africanus,
of Perseus by Aemilius Paullus. The senators knew their
Roman history and they had taken the point. Tacitus con-
ceals it. For Syphax and Perseus were not only kings exhi-
bited at the most glorious triumphs of the old Republic.
They were also outstanding examples of the mutability of
human affairs, moving their noble Roman conquerors to
compassion, and causing them to reflect on the need for
moderation and clemency. When Syphax was brought into

the Roman camp 'even Scipio was moved by the contrast between his former prosperity and his present lot ...'.[59] Still more striking was the case of Perseus, a greater king and of a more famous race, as told by Livy and, on a more ample scale, by Plutarch. Paullus rose to meet Perseus, shedding tears, as he was brought into his headquarters. But Perseus abased himself with shameful entreaties (unlike Caratacus!), and met the stern reproach that courage in misfortune brings praise even from enemies, but that the Romans consider cowardice, even if successful, the most disgraceful of qualities. Then Paullus spoke of fortune and of human affairs, and called on the young men of his staff to abandon empty insolence and the pride of victory. Livy also relates how Paullus tried to comfort Perseus with the thought that 'the clemency of the Roman people, proven in the disasters of so many kings and peoples, offers you not merely a hope but almost a firm guarantee of safety'. For Caratacus, of course, it was *clementia principis* and not *clementia populi Romani*; but it was subtle on the part of the Senate to set Claudius side by side with the high-souled heroes of the Republic. No compliment could have been more acceptable to an Emperor with his veneration for the Roman past, himself the pupil of Livy.

How the eight years of operations in Britain were made use of by official propaganda will now be clear. In words that we have used elsewhere : 'A Roman expedition, well-officered and brilliantly led, crosses the Ocean and lands in Britain, smashing barriers which we have called both geographical and psychological. When the Emperor takes the field in person, the most powerful state in Britain is quickly defeated. The resistance of other British states is usually short-lived, though sharp in the south-west. A British province takes shape, buttressed by client kingdoms whose loyalty stands up under stress. Only in Wales, under Caratacus, is resistance prolonged. When at last that prince is overcome, there is a notable display of Imperial *clementia* to a gallant adversary. The recklessness of Caesar, the fiasco of Gaius, are not repeated. There is a break with the inertia of Tiberius. Throughout the model is Augustus. The bounds of the Empire are extended to the western limit of the known world, and the sacred *pomoerium* of Rome enlarged by an Emperor whose *pietas* has once again placed her in the right relationship with the gods.'

## 6  Wars against the Silures and the Brigantes
### AD 51–57

The impressive picture built up by Roman propaganda had a serious flaw. It was not accepted in the lands west of the Severn. The Silures were unappeased and unsubdued. Stung by the loss of Caratacus, they took the field again, and 'as if to avenge the death of so great a king', waged a relentless and brilliant guerrilla warfare that brought Ostorius Scapula to his grave. His successor, Didius Gallus, made no advances in Wales, and was faced with troubles in Brigantia, for which he achieved only a temporary solution. The last phase of the Claudian Conquest of Britain is thus marked by setbacks and loss of momentum. These produced a disillusion with the whole British venture so acute that, early in the reign of Nero, serious consideration was given to abandoning the new province. Not until AD 57 was a decision made to go forward, and it implies a throwing overboard of the Claudian policy of limited conquest in the lowland zone of Britain for a new design involving the conquest of Wales. Events in Britain and elsewhere were to postpone its realization for a further twenty years. Quintus Veranius, the governor appointed to put the Neronian forward policy into

operation, died in his first year of office. His successor,
Suetonius Paulinus, was on the point of completing the conquest of North Wales when the great rebellion led by
Boudicca (AD 60) broke out in his rear, and the province was
almost lost. The governors who had to deal with its aftermath were compelled to think in terms of reconstruction
and reform, rather than of conquest. Then came the civil
wars of AD 69. Not until Vespasian was firmly in control
could Rome produce splendid armies and great generals,
Petilius Cerialis, Julius Frontinus, and Julius Agricola, who
would lead them forward once more into the highland zone,
and attempt the conquest of Caledonia.

It is worth looking ahead to see the whole pattern of
events to follow. But our concern here is with the first five
years only, AD 52–7, and with the work of the last two governors appointed by Claudius. Once again, we are wholly dependent on Tacitus, and for a story which he does not choose
to tell at length. The campaigns of these years were indecisive, devoid of incidents gratifying to Roman pride, like
the last stand of Caratacus. Didius Gallus, elderly and disinclined for further exertion, belongs to that class of governor of Britain whom Tacitus regarded with contempt. Yet
we can discern in his narrative,[1] for all its compression,
events as dramatic as any we have yet encountered, and
marked with the added interest of British success.

The renewal of hostilities by the Silures clearly took by
surprise the Roman Army and its high command. Ostorius
had supposed that their fighting spirit was broken by the defeat of Caratacus, and that he could now keep them under
control by building a network of forts in their territory. A
substantial number of legionary cohorts were detailed for
these duties, protected by auxiliary units; the rest of the
legion's forces were presumably withdrawn to their bases at
Gloucester and (perhaps) Wall. The first sign of trouble was
an attack on the temporary camp of one of these construction parties, under the command of a *praefectus castrorum.*

The Silurian force was large enough to have carried the Roman position and massacred its defenders, but messengers had got through to the nearest forts and help arrived in the nick of time. As it was, the commanding officer, eight centurions, and, to use Tacitus' words, 'the bravest fighters from the ranks' were killed – a striking success for the Silures. It was soon followed by another action, which might well rank among the most important battles of the whole Claudian invasion if a full account of it had been given by Tacitus. It began with a Silurian attack on a Roman foraging party, which was put to flight, along with cavalry squadrons sent to their support. Ostorius himself now took a hand, sending in infantry reinforcements. These, too, failed to check the Roman rout, and the main strength of at least two legions had to be flung in. First the position was stabilized, then the Romans got the upper hand : but by now the day was far advanced and the enemy (significant phrase !) 'got away with only slight loss'. Encouraged by their success, the Silures now passed over to a general offensive. This next phase was marked by frequent engagements and – perhaps even more telling – by widespread guerrilla warfare, vividly described by Tacitus. 'More often they crept through the glens and swamps like bandits – each man as chance offered or courage led, accidentally or deliberately, for booty or for revenge, at the command of their leaders – or sometimes, without their knowledge.'

No place names are given for any of the events described above, except that the first action took place 'in the territory of the Silures', as presumably did all the others. The modern reader will hardly be content if no effort is made to place them on the map. Clyro, one may suggest, could very well be the scene of the first action. To control the Silures it would be essential to hold the Wye Valley, and this large fort, now believed to contain traces of Claudian occupation,[2] is, in size and position, most suitable as the base for a large construction party sent out from Gloucester under a camp commandant. It is less easy to suggest the 'nearest forts' from which help was sent. The nearest fort may have been at Kenchester. Abergavenny was about twenty and Usk and Llandovery each about thirty-five miles away. There may, of course, have been other forts on the Black Mountain fringes, built in the earlier campaigns against Caratacus, whose sites we do not know.[3] For the second and bigger action, a clue would be provided if we could be sure that it took place within half a day's march of a main legionary base. This could only be at Gloucester. But it is more likely that by now Ostorius was in the field at the head of an expeditionary force : the mention of two legions is strong support for this view. The 'glens and swamps' of the guerrilla phase could well be the wooded hills of the Forest of Dean and the marshes of the lower Severn, through which raiding parties of the Silures could find their way into the Roman province.

Tacitus, however, is usually more interested in the mood of the combatants than the place of the action. He leaves us in no doubt of Ostorius' feelings at this juncture – they were that mixture of exasperation and fury which seems in all ages an occupational hazard of the high command. A year ago he had been voted triumphal honours for a war that he was supposed to have won : now he looked like losing it. The military situation was alarming : worse still, he was made to look ridiculous. Tacitus has a sarcastic comment on the premature triumphal honours decreed to supposed conquerors of the Numidian chief Tacfarinas in the reign of Tiberius – 'there were already three laurelled statues in Rome, yet Tacfarinas was still plundering Africa'.[4] Remarks of this kind may have been let fall incautiously over the wine in mess at Gloucester. It is under such circumstances that a general's mind will turn to thoughts of extermination, and so it was with Ostorius. 'The very name of the Silures', he declared, must be completely wiped out, as happened to the Sugambri, who were either massacred or transported to Gaul!'[5]

The choice of example is illuminating, for it recalls a notable piece of Roman ruthlessness (*atrocitas*) in dealing with a barbarian people. The Sugambri, a hostile people living on the east bank of the Rhine, had, in the reign of Augustus, first to suffer a reduction of their fighting strength in their own lands, and were then transported into Gallia Belgica, where they lost their tribal identity. Their men were taken away to fight as auxiliaries in the Roman Army; although the name Sugambri continues to appear on military inscriptions down to the second century AD, it signifies little more than the name of the unit. As a political entity, the Sugambri had ceased to exist. It was a ruthless solution – as ruthless as anything applied in modern times to the American Indian. The general's purpose became known to the Silures – through prisoners, deserters, or spies? – and, not surprisingly, did nothing to diminish the 'peculiar stubbornness' (*praecipua pervicacia*) of that people.[6]

In the grimmer phase that had now developed it was the Silures who struck the next blow. Two Roman auxiliary units, engaged on ravaging their territory, failed to take the precautions needed against so bold and nimble an enemy. They were surrounded, and either killed or taken prisoner. It is tempting to read Tacitus' *incautius* in a geographical sense, and to suppose that they had gone too far into enemy territory, beyond the range of Roman support which saved the situation in our two earlier instances – a penetration, perhaps, into the Plain of Gwent? The defeated Romans were more useful alive than dead, for we are told that 'by distributing among them spoils and prisoners the Silures were inciting other British tribes to rebellion' (*ceteras quoque nationes ad defectionem trahebant*). The word *defectio*, if taken strictly, would suggest tribes within the Roman province – unless some sort of agreement had been reached with the other three tribes of Wales after the defeat of Caratacus. In any case, it is clear that the successes of the Silures had encouraged anti-Roman elements everywhere, and that a new and formidable native confederacy was taking shape.

*Atrocitas* might suit the needs of the hour, but it was not destined to be put into practice in South Wales. For it was

Ostorius who died 'worn out with the burden of his cares'.
Tacitus does not fail to record the joy of the Silures, who
took pride in the thought that they had 'destroyed a formidable adversary, if not in battle, then at least in the course
of war'. They were entitled to congratulate themselves. We,
too, should pause at this moment of success for the Silures,
to reflect that we do not know the name of a single one of
their leaders. This is a pity, because as 'patriot chiefs' they
take rank beside Caratacus and Boudicca; indeed, the successes they won against the Roman Army in the field are
unparalleled by any British people before the wars of the
second century AD in Caledonia and Brigantia. As a result of
their efforts against Ostorius, their people retained their
identity, to become, in the end, a *civitas* of the Roman province. Their descendants still live in the land, and, though
their name is now used only in a specialist context,[7] those
who go to play Rugby football in South Wales will testify
that their *pervicacia* is well maintained.

The death of Ostorius at this juncture meant a grave
emergency for the Roman government, reflected in Tacitus'
words 'when the death of the Governor became known,
Claudius sent in his place [*suffecit*] Aulus Didius [Gallus] lest
the province should be without a ruler'. The statement is less
straightforward than might appear, for it is obvious that
Britain must have a governor : to labour the point is to suggest that the emergency explains, but does not justify, the
choice of Didius Gallus. We are primed for the disparaging
comments which, on no fewer than four occasions, Tacitus
goes out of his way to make on Didius' conduct of British
affairs. And what is the point of *suffecit*, since that verb
is normally used of appointments made to an office whose
holder's term has not expired ? It implies, perhaps, that
Ostorius was due to retire in 53, and that one of the consuls
of 52 was already marked to succeed him. For some reason
this man could not be released on Ostorius' death, but Didius
Gallus was in Rome and available, though at his age he
would not normally have expected another provincial com-

mand. History and epigraphy tell us enough of the career of
the third Governor of Britain to discount some of Tacitus'
settled bias against him. *Consul suffectus* in AD 36, he probably accompanied Claudius to Britain in AD 43, and may
have held a special cavalry command. His next appointment
took him from the north-west to the north-east of the Roman
Empire, for he became Governor of Moesia. As such he had
to deal with troubles in two client-kingdoms, Thrace and
Bosporus. In both a mixture of war and diplomacy produced
a solution favourable to Rome, and Didius was awarded
*ornamenta triumphalia*. Later he held a senatorial province
but it was this Moesian command which made him a good
appointment for Britain at this time. Tacitus, it should be
admitted, is not his only critic, for there is a story in Quintilian[8] of a rebuke administered to him as being more concerned for his own interests, rather than those of the State, in
canvassing with excessive zeal for a provincial command,
which could well have been that of Britain at the death of
Ostorius.

Certainly Didius, by the year AD 52, was 'full of honours',
but if this made him indolent it did not appear at the outset.
Hastening to Britain, he found that the situation, bad
enough at the death of Ostorius, had deteriorated further,
and was now out of military control. The Silures had defeated a legion, 'under the command of Manlius Valens' –
and presumably the XXth – and now they were ravaging far
and wide in the province. In other words, the defences along
the lower Severn had collapsed, and the Roman units were
pinned within their forts, as they were to be later in the
early phase of Boudicca's rebellion. (The name of the commander is given with a purpose. The defeat by the Silures
would seem to have damaged Manlius Valens' whole career.
In AD 69 he is still no more than a legionary commander – the
oldest known. He was to go on to a second and more notable
record, for in AD 96 he became the oldest man ever to
hold the consulship – at the age of 89!)[9] Tacitus is at pains
to play down the situation – 'the report [of the defeat]', he

says, 'was exaggerated, first by the enemy to alarm the in-
coming governor, and secondly by Didius ... so as to gain
greater credit if he settled the situation, and to have a better
excuse, if it persisted.' To this tangle of motives we may
fairly add another – the desire of Tacitus to discredit Didius.
Perhaps Manlius Valens was his source? Tacitus was consul
in AD 97; he may well have heard the old gentleman, still
embittered over memories of the débâcle in Britain more
than forty years ago. Even so, Tacitus cannot deny that
Didius achieved a rapid solution. 'On his arrival the Silures
were expelled from the province.' Since we do not hear of
them again for four or five years, it would seem that they
took a hard knock in the process. And if Didius made no
gains in Silurian territory as a result, he may only have been
obeying instructions. In any case, two unforeseen and serious
events ruled out any adventures in Wales during his term of
office.

The first of these was the murder of Claudius at the in-
stigation of his wife Agrippina in AD 54. It brought to power
a new administration under a young and untried *princeps* :
some of Claudius' policies, and many of his advisers, were
discarded. Prominent among the latter was Narcissus, who
had been so closely identified with the invasion of Britain.
The current line in imperial propaganda was to portray
Nero as the new Augustus; a return to the Augustan frontiers would have been in keeping with this policy. Here, in
the early years of Nero, is the best context for Suetonius'
statement that that emperor once contemplated a withdrawal from Britain. Didius Gallus, obviously, could make
no forward move until this cardinal decision had been made.
The remainder of his office would presumably have been
quiet, but for events beyond his control in Brigantia. Queen
Cartimandua had been well paid for her loyalty to Rome
when she handed over Caratacus. She gained wealth, as one
might expect, but Tacitus is at pains to emphasize that she
also gained power (*auxerat potentiam*).[10] This suggests an
expansion of the southern kingdom, over which Cartiman-

dua ruled directly, at the expense of the northern Brigantian realm of her husband Venutius. It is unlikely, however, that she gained in the respect of her subjects, and Venutius' resentment, combined with that of the anti-Roman faction in the state, led to an outburst of civil war that called for Roman intervention. It is unfortunate that Tacitus did not choose to work up the Cartimandua story, but he discloses enough to show that it had all the makings of a great Celtic heroic tale. Cartimandua was wealthy and cruel, lustful and treacherous – a Clytemnestra of a woman. She had captured Caratacus by guile, now she employed the same deceitful arts to get Venutius' brother and kinsmen in her power. Venutius himself was a formidable figure – the greatest military chieftain in Britain, now that Caratacus was gone.[11] He could plan boldly and muster a great force – witness the enormous earthworks at Stanwick (137 acres, later enlarged to over 600), where his followers gathered in the last phases of the struggle for Brigantian independence.[12] Cartimandua's insolence, and this latest aggression were more than he could stomach, even though it brought him into collision with Rome. And now his reaction was swift and characteristic : 'a powerful band of young warriors' – the royal war-band, in fact – 'invaded her kingdom',[13] the object being, no doubt, to rescue Venutius' kinsmen, and perhaps to capture the Queen. The heroic world of northern Britain was much the same five centuries later, when the *teulu* or war-band of Mynyddwg Mwynfawr, lord of Edinburgh, 'went to Catraeth' to make their famous raid on the English settled at Catterick in the ruins of the old Roman town. Thanks to the poet Aneirin, we know much of their deeds – 'three hundred warriors went to Catraeth, and of all that host but one man came back alive'.[14] But – 'they killed seven times their number of English'.

How many were in the war-band of Venutius we cannot say, but its movements were known to the Roman command, and help was ready for Cartimandua when the situation looked like getting out of hand. Didius Gallus by now was too infirm for campaigning in the Pennines, which dates the Brigantian civil war late in his governorship, in 55, or more probably 56. He was forced to act through subordinates, which meant that operations were in charge of the legionary commander Caesius Nasica. Again, the name has significance, for Caesius Nasica was probably the brother of Petilius Cerialis, who later (*c* AD 60) held the same command at Lincoln, and as governor of Britain carried out the conquest of the Brigantes (71–4).[15] His command was, almost certainly, the IXth Legion, and the campaigns that follow are the first in which we can identify that legion in action. It was thought at first that auxiliary units would be sufficient, but those sent to support the Queen had to fight a fierce action, which only in its last phases went in their favour. Their victory – if such it was – did not end the campaign, and the legion itself had to take the field and fight another hard battle. Since the war-band can hardly have been numerous enough to face a Roman legion, it looks as though Venutius had followed up with his main army. This is all that Tacitus has to tell about the military side of the war against the Brigantes, and of the diplomatic sequel he says nothing. Yet once more, as with the Silures, a satisfactory solution was apparently reached. Cartimandua retained her kingdom, and Venutius his : for the war had begun as a Brigantian affair, not as a move against Rome. Even their divorce was some years in the future, and if Venutius by now cherished a vendetta against Cartimandua and a hatred for Rome,[16] he had to wait to express them until an hour of graver weakness than Didius Gallus can have foreseen. The crucial test, surely, of the settlement lay in the fact that when the rebellion of Boudicca broke out only a few years later, Cartimandua was able to prevent her people from going over to the rebel cause. The Brigantian problem was the last that Didius Gallus handled in a long and honourable career : there is no indication that he bungled it.

If it was hard to place the events in South Wales on the map, it is harder still here in the north. If we could be sure

that Cartimandua's capital was at the northern Camulodunum (Almondbury), it is somewhere near the modern
Huddersfield that we should look for the scene of the fierce
action between the Brigantian war-band and the Roman
auxiliaries. As for the legionary battle, the Brigantian fortress at Stanwick and the Roman legionary base at York were
both later to attest to the importance of the natural line of
penetration along the east flank of the Pennines. Somewhere between York and Catterick would be the likely scene
of the battle where Caesius Nasica met and turned back the
army of the northern king.

One further feature of Didius Gallus' work may be deduced from Tacitus. In the *Agricola* he makes the familiar
charge that Didius Gallus did no more than maintain the
ground won by his predecessors, adding the contemptuous
phrase that 'by founding a small number of forts in the re-
moter parts of the province he sought to win a reputation for
having enlarged the duty entrusted to him'.[17] Now it seems
unlikely that Didius Gallus can have retained, let alone extended, the system of forts in Silurian territory built up by
Scapula. But the situation in Brigantia at the end of Didius'
term of office would seem to demand just such an extension
as Tacitus has described. There are signs of an early fort
at Little Chester,[18] and certainly that place was a nodal
point in the later system of roads and forts in the Peak. But
the object of this system was to control the native peoples
of the Peak, and to protect the rear of the strategic road con-
necting the legionary bases at York and Chester. To protect
the kingdom of Cartimandua against an attack from the
north it would be imperative to have a firm grip on the Ouse
Valley. Here again one thinks of York, which has yielded
some pre-Flavian objects, which may indicate military occupation earlier than the legionary fortress of AD 71.[19] Didius
Gallus may well have been the first Roman governor to
realize the importance of this great strategic centre of the
north. North Lincolnshire was already in Roman hands
presumably up to the Trent and Humber and one should

seek evidence for this northern advance on the road leading
north-west from Lincoln to the Pennine fringe, and marked
by later forts at Bawtry, Doncaster, and Castleford. A little
to the south-west of this line the fort at Templeborough has
been dated to about AD 60.[20]

There is a twenty-three acre fort at Rossington Bridge
near Doncaster,[21] so far undated, and the considerable
amount of excavation at Brough-on-Humber has produced
no hint of anything earlier than AD 71.[22] More significant
probably is the twenty-five acre fort at Newton on the east
bank of the Trent, discovered by Dr St Joseph in 1962. It
was linked by him to the Longthorpe fort in the Nene [23] and
his suggestion of the division of *Legio* IX in the earlier phase
of the conquest has been accepted by Professor Frere.[24] These
forts are certainly very similar in plan and it is a very neat
theory, but the time for the Romans to need a legionary
reserve at this point on the Trent seems to fit the troubles of
Brigantia under Gallus better than earlier situations, but
again one must await excavations.[25] A possible small fort has
been noted by Dr St Joseph at Sawley, eight and a half
miles to the north-west of Little Chester.[26]

While these events were taking place in Brigantia, the
government of Nero had reached its decision about Britain.
There was to be no withdrawal. Its implications were that
the Claudian policy of limited conquests in the lowland zone
of England would have to be discarded. Confronted with the
geographical and political realities of Britain, it had shown itself to be inadequate. The security of the province would demand at least the conquest of Wales; flaws had shown themselves in the policy of supporting a client-kingdom in
Brigantia, but for the time it would be allowed to stand. A
new governor would clearly be needed, and with the hour
came the man. Quintus Veranius, in his mid-forties, with a
fine military record in Lycia and Pamphylia, viewed his task
with enthusiasm and confidence – and was destined to die
within a year.[27]

We have already reviewed the many checks and delays

encountered by the Neronian forward policy, which was not
to be implemented until the succession of able governors
under Vespasian. Thus the problems of Wales and Brigantia
remained open for almost two decades after Claudius. With
the Eighties came Agricola's audacious but unsuccessful project for the conquest of Caledonia. Once this was abandoned
a northern *limes* had to be established – hence the vast and
expensive schemes of Hadrian and Antoninus Pius. Behind
these barriers the Roman province prospered until the
troubles of the later fourth century. Even so, this northern
British *limes* was always one of the most warlike frontiers of
the Empire, and was breached several times. Add to all this
the known troubles in Brigantia in the second century. The
example of Caratacus was not in vain. At all times in Britain,
within and without the Roman province, there were to be
men who preferred *libertas* to *pax*.

# APPENDIX I

## *The Narrative of Dio Cassius, LX, 19–22*

§19. . . . At about this time Aulus Plautius, a distinguished Senator, commanded an expedition to Britain. For a certain Bericus, expelled from the island by internal strife, had persuaded Claudius to dispatch a force there. That is how Aulus Plautius came to command an invading army, but it was with great difficulty that he led his army out of Gaul. The soldiers grumbled at having to campaign outside the inhabited world (as they put it), and they refused to listen to him until Narcissus, who had been sent by Claudius, mounted the commander's platform and began to address them. At this point they were still more annoyed with Aulus Plautius and disinclined to let Narcissus utter a word; but all of a sudden they shouted out aloud the well-known cry 'Io Saturnalia!' (this because at the festival of Saturn the slaves dress up in their masters' clothes to keep holiday). After this they readily obeyed Plautius' orders. But the delay had postponed their sailing-date until late in the season: they sailed in three divisions to avoid the delays in landing which might be occasioned by the ferrying over of a single force. Their crossing was at first discouraging because contrary winds drove them back, but eventually they were

cheered by a brilliant flash of light which appeared in the
east and shot across the sky to the west – the direction of their
course. They landed on the island without opposition, for the
reports which reached the Britons had led them to suppose
that the Romans would not come – consequently they had
not mustered. Even at this stage they declined to meet them
in the field, but took refuge in the swamps and forests, hoping in this way so to wear them down that they would sail
away with nothing achieved – precisely as had happened in
the case of Julius Caesar.

§ 20. Aulus Plautius therefore had much trouble in making
contact with them. When he did so, he defeated first Caratacus and then Togodumnus, the sons of Cunobelinus, who
was dead. (At this period the Britons were not free and independent, but ruled by the kings of other tribes.) When these
kings had fled he won over by agreement a portion of the
Bodunni [*sic*], a people dependent on the Catuvellauni;
thereupon he left a garrison there and continued his advance. Then he came to a river. The Britons supposed that
the Romans would not be able to cross it without a bridge,
and so had encamped carelessly on the opposite bank. He
therefore sent across Gallic troops who were trained to swim
with full equipment across the swiftest of rivers. Surprise was
achieved against the enemy by this attack; but they did not
shoot at the men themselves; instead, wounding the horses
that drew their chariots, they made it impossible even for the
charioteers to get away in the subsequent confusion. At this
point Plautius sent over Vespasian (the future Emperor), and
his brother Sabinus, who was serving under his command. This
force also succeeded in crossing the river, and killing many
of the barbarians, who were not expecting them. The rest of
the British forces did not retreat, however, but remained to
fight on the following day. There was an indecisive struggle,
but at last Gnaeus Hosidius Geta (after being almost taken
prisoner) managed to defeat them. For this achievement he
was later awarded *ornamenta triumphalia*, though he had
never been consul. Then the Britons fell back from this posi-

tion on to the River Thames, at a point where it enters the sea and forms a large pool at high tide. Knowing the firm ground and the fords with much precision, they crossed the river without difficulty, but the Roman forces were not so successful. However, the Celts (ie auxiliaries) swam across again, and some others got over by a bridge a little way upstream, after which they assailed the barbarians from several sides at once and cut down many of them. But they were incautious in their pursuit of the rest, got themselves trapped in impassable marshes, and lost many of their men.

§ 21. Shortly after this Togodumnus died. Far from giving in, the Britons gathered all the more stubbornly to avenge him. Plautius became alarmed and refused to advance further. Resolved to hold on to ground he had already won, he sent for Claudius. Indeed, his instructions had been to do precisely this if anything untoward should happen : substantial preparation had been made for reinforcements, including troops and elephants.

When the message reached him, Claudius entrusted affairs at Rome (including the command of the troops, ie that part of the Praetorian Guard left in Rome, its commander Rufrius Pollio accompanying Claudius to Britain) to his colleague in the consulship, Lucius Vitellius, who like himself had served a full six months in office, and set out for the campaign. Sailing down the river to Ostia, he voyaged thence to Massilia; then he went across Gaul by road and river to the Ocean. Crossing the Channel, he joined the troops who had been awaiting him on the Thames. Taking them with him he crossed the river, engaged the barbarians who had gathered to dispute his advance, gained the victory, and captured Camulodunon, the royal seat of Cunobelinus. Later he won over numerous tribes —some by battle, some by negotiation — and was hailed 'imperator' several times – contrary to custom, for the rule was that none should receive this acclamation more than once in any one campaign. Disarming these tribes, he handed them over to Aulus Plautius, who received instructions to subdue the remainder of the country. He then left for Rome, having sent ahead news of his victory by Magnus and Silanus, his sons-in-law.

§ 22. On hearing of his achievement the Senate voted him the title of Britannicus, and gave permission for him to celebrate a Triumph. They further approved an annual festival of commemoration and the erection of two triumphal arches, one in Rome, and one in Gaul at the place where he crossed over to Britain. The title of Britannicus was also conferred on his son : indeed, it became his usual name. Messalina received the same seat of honour at the theatre that had been granted to Livia, and also the privilege of using a town carriage.*

* The *carpentum* was a covered carriage. Only the Empress and the Vestal Virgins had the privilege of using it, as an exception from the traffic regulations forbidding the use of wheeled vehicles in the city during daylight hours.

# APPENDIX II

## *The Chichester Inscription*

The Chichester inscription, on a Purbeck marble slab 5 ft 3 in by 2 ft 7 in, was found in four pieces which have since suffered from weathering and damage, and reads as follows* :

N]EPTVNO ET MINERVAE
   TEMPLVM
PR]O SALVTE DO[MVS] DIVINAE
EX] AVCTORITAT[E T]I CLAVD
CO]GIDVBNI R LE[GATI AVG IN BRIT
COLLE]GIVM FABROR ET [QV]I IN EO
SVNT] D S D DONANTE AREAM
. . . ]ENTE PVDENTINI FIL

*Expanded form:*

NEPTVNO ET MINERVAE
   TEMPLVM
PRO SALVTE DOMVS DIVINAE
EX AVCTORITATE TI(BERII) CLAVDII

---

\* This reading was suggested by R. G. Collingwood (Tacitus, *de vita Agricolae*, ed. Furneaux, revised by J. G. C. Anderson, 1922, 79; see also *V.C.H., Sussex*, iii, 1935, 13 and *R.I.B.*, 91).

COGIDVBNI R(EGIS) LEGAT(I) AVG(VSTI) IN
BRIT(ANNIA)
COLLEGIVM FABRORVM ET QVI IN EO
SVNT DE SVO DEDERVNT DONANTE AREAM
₅... ]ENTE PVDENTINI FILIO

*Meaning:*
A temple to Neptune, Minerva and for the well-being of the
Divine House (of the Emperor) by the authority of King
Tiberius Claudius Cogidubnus Imperial Legate in Britain
(erected by) the guild of artisans and its members at their
own cost. . . . ]ens son of Pudentinus donated the site.

# APPENDIX III

## *The Dedicatory Inscription (C.I.L. VI 920) on the Arch of Claudius*

The restoration of this inscription is illustrated on p. 166.*
The translation is as follows :

> To the Emperor Tiberius Claudius, son of Drusus,
> Caesar Augustus Germanicus, Pontifex Maximus, Tri-
> bunician power for the eleventh time, Consul for the
> fifth time, saluted as Imperator twenty two (?) times,
> Censor, Father of his Country. [Set up by] the Senate
> and People of Rome because he received the formal sub-
> mission of eleven Kings of the Britons, overcome with
> out any loss, and because he was the first to bring bar-
> barian peoples across the Ocean under the sway of the
> Roman people.

Three points concern us here : the eleven British kings, the
phrase *sine ulla iactura*, and the reference to the Ocean. The
figure of XI is certain, the problem is to identify the British
kings concerned. Caratacus can hardly be included. He had

---

* See further, F. Castagnoli, *Bolletino della Commissione Archeo-
logica del Governatoro di Roma*, LXX (1942), pp 57–82; D. R.
Dudley, *University of Birmingham Historical Journal* VII, no 1
(1959), 11 ff.

TI·CLAVDIO·DRVSI·F·CAISARI
AVGVSTO·GERMANICO
PONTIFICI·MAXIM·TRIB·POTESTAT·XI
COS·V·IMP·XXII·CENS·PATRI·PATRIAI
SENATVS·POPVLVSQVE·ROMANVSQVOD
REGES·BRITANNORVM·XI·DEVICTOS·SINE
VLLA·IACTVRA·IN·DEDITIONEM·ACCEPERIT
GENTESQVE·BARBARAS·TRANS·OCEANVM
PRIMVS·IN·DICIONEM·POPVLI·ROMANI·REDEGERIT

been defeated before the dedication of the Arch (AD 52), but the phrase *sine ulla iactura* loses meaning if it has to cover the man who, in Tacitus' words, 'had defied Roman power for so many years'. Nor can we safely suppose the words that *devictos . . . in deditionem acceperit* apply only to those defeated in battle : they are used of formal acts of submission, whether voluntary or after defeat in war. The eleven kings named therefore appear to be those who, whether after defeat or negotiation, made their surrender in person to Claudius at Colchester. Presumably they include Cogidubnus, Prasutagus (or another king of the Iceni,) and the ruler of the Brigantes (Cartimandua?). Kings of the Coritani and Dobunni may also be suggested : perhaps too there were rulers to surrender on behalf of the Catuvellauni and Trinovantes; the Kentish tribes, the Cornovii, and the Parisii are also possibles. All we can really say is that the XI of the inscription is the kind of figure to be expected from what we know of the campaigns. The word *iactura* appears to be deliberately chosen as a word of wide meaning, and the whole phrase, taken closely with the surrender of the eleven kings, is to imply that Claudius' conduct of operations in Britain met with no reverse or setback. There is little doubt that it is meant to point the contrast with the fiasco of Gaius, exactly as the arch of Claudius at Gesoriacum (Boulogne) commemorates an authentic victory in the traditional Roman manner, in contrast to the 'lighthouse' (or trophy?) of Gaius. The claim that Claudius was the 'first to bring barbarian peoples across the Ocean under the sway of the Roman people' is a simple statement of fact, if we take it to refer to the establishment of a Roman province in Britain. A passage from Claudius' 'Speech to the Gauls' * makes it clear that the Emperor saw this as the culminating achievement of Roman history : 'I am afraid that . . . if I mention the wars we have successfully undertaken, I shall seem too immoderate, in having sought to make a display of the glory we have won by extending the Empire across the Ocean'. Scramuzza† has shown in detail how these British conquests of Claudius round off the work of his kinsmen in the lands surrounding the North Sea.

It should be added that the Arch at Cyzicus : *C.I.L.*, III, S. 7061 (=Dessau *I.L.S.*, 217), set up for reasons of local politics, selects only the surrender of the eleven kings, and says nothing about the 'Conquest of the Ocean'.

* M. P. Charlesworth, *Documents to illustrate the reigns of Claudius and Nero* (Cambridge, 1939), 9.
† V. Scramuzza, *The Emperor Claudius*, 205, 308.

# APPENDIX IV

## Military Tombstones

1 *Two military tombstones from Colchester (2 and 4)*
Found in 1884 in Beverley Road along the presumed
course of the Roman road from London. It reads:

M(ARCVS)  FAVONI(VS)  M(ARCI)  F(ILIVS)
   POL(LIA) FACI
LIS · > LEG(IONIS) XX · VERECVND
VS ET NOVICIVS LIB(ERTI) POS
ERVNT · H(IC) S(ITVS) E(ST)

Marcus Favonius Facilis, son of Marcus, of the Pollian
tribe, centurion of the XXth Legion, erected by Verecun-
dus and Novicius his freedmen. He is buried here. (*C.I.L.*,
vii, 90; *R.I.B.*, 200).

2 Found in 1928 in Beverley Road near the site of the above
where early graves have been noted (*Roman Colchester*,
1959, p 251). The inscription below the relief tells us that
it is the tombstone of Longinus, son of Sdapezematygus, a
*duplicarius* of the first Thracian *ala*, born in Sardica (now
Sofia in Bulgaria), died in his fortieth year and fifteenth
year of service. He wears a jerkin of large scales and his

sturdy horse is finely caparisoned. The stone suffered damage, presumably in the revolt of Boudicca in AD 60 when the face was smashed, the lance knocked off and the stone overthrown. (*J.R.S.*, 18 (1928), p 212; *Trans. Essex Arch. Soc.*, 19.2, pp 1–6.)

3 *A legionary tombstone from Mainz* (5)
It reads :

P(UBLIUS) FLAVOLEIUS . P(UBLII) . F(ILIUS) .
  POL(LIA) .
MUTINA . CORDUS . MIL(ES) .
LEG(IONIS) . XIIII . GEM(INAE) . H(IC) . S(ITUS) .
  E(ST) ,
ANN(ORUM) . XLIII . STIP(ENDIORUM) . XXIII .
  C(AIUS) .
VIBENNIUS . L(UCII) . F(ILIUS) .
  EX . T(ESTAMENTO) . FEC(IT)

Publius Flavoleius Cordus, son of Publius, of the Pollian tribe, born at Mutina (Modena in Northern Italy), soldier of the XIVth Legion *Gemina*. He is buried here. 43 years old, 23 years service. Erected by Caius Vibennius, son of Lucius, according to the provisions of the will (*C.I.L.*, xiii, 7255.)

Cordus is shown in his undress uniform holding his *pilum*, which has suffered damage, and a scroll, presumably denoting his citizenship. Details of the dagger (*pugio*) and military belt are very clear. The shield slung on his back is the mason's representation of the normal semi-cylindrical type.

4 *A military tombstone from Cirencester*
Found in 1836 in Watermoor to the south of the Roman town. (*Arch.* 27, 215; 69, 186; *C.I.L.*, vii, 68.) The inscription tells us that the tombstone is that of Sextus Valerius

Genialis, a trooper of a Thracian *ala*, born in Frisia (now north-eastern Holland). Although Genialis is described as a trooper (*eques*) he carries in addition to the oval shield a device which appears to be some kind of standard but not the usual cavalry flag (*vexillum*). He wears an elaborate helmet but damage to the stone prevents it being positively identified as one of those used on parade, with a face-visor similar to that from Ribchester in the British Museum (*Art in Roman Britain*, 1962, No 108). On his jerkin is an emblem which may have represented a Medusa head, thought to give protection.

5 *Three military tombstones from Wroxeter*
Found in 1752 in a field nearly a mile from Wroxeter village, about 200 yards from the foundation of the Roman town wall on the north-east towards Watling Street. It reads :

M(ARCVS)    PETRONIVS    L(VCII)    F(ILIVS)
MEN(ENIA TRIBV)    VIC(ETIA).    ANN(ORVM)
XXXVIII MIL(ES)
LEG(IONIS)    XIIII    GEM(INAE)    MILITAVIT
    ANN(OS) XVIII
SIGN(IFER) FVIT H(IC) S(ITVS) E(ST).

Marcus Petronius, son of Lucius, of the Menenian tribe (all Roman citizens belonged to a tribe for voting purposes), born at Vicetia (Vicenza, in Northern Italy), 38 years old, a soldier of the XIVth Legion *Gemina.* He served 18 years, he was a standard bearer. He is buried here. (*C.I.L.*, vii, 155; *R.I.B.*, 294.)

6 Found with No 5 and reads :

C(AIVS)    MANNIVS    C(AI)    F(ILIVS)    POL(LIA)
SECVNDVS    POLLEN(TIA)    MIL(ES)    LEG(IONIS)
XX AN(N)ORV(M)    LII

STIP(ENDIORVM)    XXXI    BEN(EFICIARIVS)
LEG(ATI) PR(O PRAETORE) H(IC) S(ITVS) E(ST)

Caius Mannius Secundus, son of Caius, of the Pollian
tribe, born at Pollentia (near Turin in Northern Italy), a
soldier of the XXth Legion, 52 years old, 31 years service,
a junior staff officer of the governor. He is buried here.
(*C.I.L.*, vii, 156; *R.I.B.*, 293.)

*Beneficarii* were normally given duties similar to those of a
District Officer or made responsible for Toll and Tax collection.

7 Found about the same time as Nos 5 and 6 and reads:

TIB(ERIVS) CLAVD(IVS) TIR[.]NTIVS EQ(VES)
COH(ORTIS) [..]
THRACVM AN[N]ORVM LVII STI[P]ENDIOR(VM)
XX[.. H(IC) S(ITVS) [E(ST)

Tiberius Claudius Tir.[.]ntius, a trooper of the (?) Cohort
of Thracians, 57 years old (?) years service. He is buried
here. (*C.I.L.*, vii, 158; *R.I.B.*, 291.)

# APPENDIX V

## *The Seven Sisters Hoard*

The Seven Sisters hoard (*15*) was found at Nant-y-Cafn in the Vale of Neath, Glamorgan, in 1875 but the collection did not finally reach the National Museum of Wales until 1904, after which it was published by Romilly Allen (*Arch. Camb.*, 1905, pp 127–46). Among the twenty objects recovered are six tankard handles and six pieces of horse gear decorated with enamel. Ten of the other items are undoubtedly of Roman military origin typical of the middle of the first century but the Celtic character of the remainder has led to the belief that much of the hoard is of native origin. (Hence it was included by W. F. Grimes in his *Guide to the Collections illustrating the Prehistory of Wales*, 1939, Fig 40 on p 195.) The poor decoration of the enamelled pieces has, however, lost much of its Celtic flavour. They are comparable to similar objects found in Roman contexts (eg Waddon Hill in Dorset, Carlisle and Inchtuthil, all as yet unpublished). It is the kind of work one might expect from British craftsmen obliged to mass-produce their wares for the Roman Army. It is suggested that the whole of this hoard may have been part of the spoils from a sacked fort or beaten cavalry unit. An exception might be made for the tankard handles but even these are not unknown in Roman forts (*Antiquities from the Hod Hill in the Durden Collection*, 1962, Fig 14, nos 1, 5 and 6 and plate X; Waddon Hill, Dorset, *Proc. Prehist. Soc.*, 17 (1952), Pl X, No 3, and *Proc. Dorset Nat. Hist. and Arch. Soc.*, 82 (1961), Fig 10; and a later example from Newstead, *A Roman Frontier Post and its People*, 1911, Pl LIV, No 7). A wooden tankard, adorned with these handles, was a useful and decorative item a Roman soldier would have purchased from a British craftsman or taken as loot.

# Notes and References

## CHAPTER I

1. If indeed the Hosidius Geta who served in Mauretania is the same person: he may have been a brother of the Geta who came to Britain
2. Caesar, *De Bello Gallico* (referred to below as *D.B.G.*), iv, 22; v, 8
3. Dessau, *Inscriptiones Latinae Selectae* (referred to below as *I.L.S.*), 970; *Année Epigraphique* (1947), No 76 and 1949, No 11
4. By Lawrence J. F. Keppie in *Britannia* 2 (1971), 149–55
5. *Classical Quarterly*, 13 (1963), 269
6. Dio Cassius, lx, 20. Tacitus frequently mentions these units, whose skill and fighting qualities seem to have impressed him
7. '*Insularum quas Romana notitia complectitur maxima*', Tacitus, *Agricola*, 10
8. *Annals*, ii, 33 ff
9. It is highly probable that some of them will have taken part in the abortive expedition of Gaius. J. P. V. Balsdon, 'Notes concerning the Principate of Gaius', *J.R.S.*, 24 (1934), 13–24
10. Dio Cassius, lx, 19
11. J. P. V. Balsdon, *J.R.S.*, 24 (1934), 17
12. G. L. Cheesman, *The Auxilia of the Roman Army* (1914)
13. There is a tiny fragment from one such inscription of the early second century from the turf section of Hadrian's Wall, recog-

nized and brilliantly interpreted by R. G. Collingwood, *Cumberland and Westmorland Trans.*, 35 (1935), 220

14. C. G. Starr, *Roman Imperial Navy 31 BC–AD 324* (2nd Ed., 1960)
15. *Annals*, ii, 6
16. Caesar, *D.B.G.*, iv, 32
17. Sir Cyril Fox, *A Find of the Early Iron Age from Llyn Cerrig Bach, Anglesey* (National Museum of Wales 1946)
18. *Ant. J.*, 27 (1947), 117–19
19. Caesar's British expeditions are described in *De Bello Gallico* iv, 20–36, and v, 8–23. The best discussion of the problems raised is still that of Rice Holmes in *Ancient Britain and the Invasions of Julius Caesar* (Oxford, 1907), though many of his views would not be accepted by modern scholars
20. See on this A. N. Sherwin-White, *Greece and Rome*, Vol IV, No 1 (Julius Caesar Bimillenary Number) 36–45
21. For possible political reasons see C. E. Stevens, *Antiquity* XXI (1947), 3–9
22. *Verulamium, A Belgic and Two Roman Cities* (1936), 16–22

CHAPTER 2

1. The Celtic name is Camulodunon
2. Iv, 5, 1–2
3. C. F. C. Hawkes and M. R. Hull, *Camulodunum* (1947)
4. Suetonius, *Caligula*, 44, 0
5. See D. F. Allen, 'The Belgic dynasties of Britain and their Coins', *Archaeologia*, 90 (1944), 1–46, and summary in the OS *Map of Southern Britain in the Iron Age*, 1962; *The Coins of the Coritani*, 1963
6. R. P. Mack, *The Coinage of Ancient Britain* (1953), no 265 and p 58. They are inscribed CARA and are identical in type to the silver issue of Epaticcus
7. Dio Cassius, lx, 19
8. Tacitus, *Agricola*, 24
9. Suetonius, *Claudius*, 17
10. *Cambridge Antiquarian Soc. Proc.*, 50 (1956), 1–27; evidence from the excavation of Wandlebury
11. See I. A. Richmond, 'The Cornovii', in *Culture and Environment* (1963), 251 ff

12. *Agricola*, 11
13. Strabo, iv, 5, 1–3. It should be noted that the *Res Gestae* of Augustus (vi, 32) records the names of two British princes, Dumnobellaunus and Tincommius, among suppliants seeking his friendship
14. By C. E. Stevens in *Aspects of Archaeology in Britain and Beyond* (1951), 340
15. Dio Cassius, lx, 23, 6
16. *Annals*, xii, 37
17. Caesar, *D.B.G.*, i, 29
18. Diodorus Siculus, v, 25
19. *Annals*, xii, 34; *Agricola*, 15
20. Strabo, iv, 2, 3
21. Probably the best modern discussion is by A. Momigliano, *Claudius* (reprinted 1961)

CHAPTER 3

1. Dio Cassius, lx, 19–22, gives a narrative of the campaign
2. *C.I.L.*, vi, 920: 31203; *C.I.L.*, iii, 7061. See further pp 185f
3. Suetonius, *Claudius*, 17; *Vespasian*, 4
4. Caesar, *D.B.G.*, iv, 25
5. Tacitus, *Agricola*, 14
6. We owe much in what follows to our discussion with Professor Birley
7. Professor Birley has pointed out (*Sussex Arch. Coll.*, 94 (1956), 102) that the first of a new series of judicial officers, C. Salvius Liberalis, was appointed to Britain *c* AD 78. This may have been as a result of the death of the king and the consequent absorption of the kingdom into the province in an equitable and peaceful manner, avoiding the holocaust at the death of Prasutagus, the King of the Iceni
8. By Professor C. F. C. Hawkes, at the suggestion of Mr C. E. Stevens, in *Bagendon, A Belgic Oppidum* (1961), 65
9. *Breviarium Historiae Romanae*, vii, 13
10. He had at the death of Gaius proposed in the Senate a return to the Republic
11. Directed by J. P. Bushe-Fox for the Society of Antiquaries, *Fourth Report on the Excavations of the Roman Fort at Richborough, Kent* (1949)

12. There is, however, a difficulty in the discovery of a gateway at the entrance. This consists of the remains of four post-pits and suggestions of two others arranged in the pattern one normally associates with a military gate. If these represent the remains of a substantial wooden structure protecting the entrance to the camp, it would appear to be of more permanent and of longer duration than our previous argument would allow. The excavator was uncertain about these finds and is at pains to point out that 'no definite proof could be obtained that these were of the same date as the Claudian defences, but they do not appear to belong to the later buildings and their central position in the entrance passage points to some connection with it'. There is yet another piece of evidence recorded by the excavator which may throw doubt on the connection of the 'gate' with the camp. The post-pits were filled with decayed turf and he states that the wooden uprights 'had been packed round with rammed sand and turf'. This could not have happened if the gate-posts had been erected as part of the original defences, since the post-pits would have been packed with the clean material dug out of the holes, and this is usually well-rammed and sterile. The presence of turf seems to indicate that the erection of this timber structure took place after the turf rampart of the camp went out of use and could be used for filling in these holes. The timbers could have belonged to the buildings subsequently erected and there is nothing in the general plan which would militate against this idea. There is yet another possibility that the turves occurred only in the trenches cut into the post-pits when the wooden uprights were removed, and this might also account for the irregular shape of the post-pits which if undisturbed are normally of neat rectangular plan. This suggestion would explain the shape of the one post-pit illustrated by a photograph

13. *Fifth Report on the Excavations of the Roman Fort at Richborough, Kent*, ed. by B. W. Cunliffe, 1968

14. *Roman Britain and the English Settlements* (2nd ed, 1937), 81

15. Professor C. F. C. Hawkes in *Bagendon, A Belgic Oppidum* (1961), 60

16. M. W. C. Hassall, 'Batavians and the Conquest of Britain', *Britannia*, 1 (1970), 131–36

17. It was not unusual for high ranking officers and officials to be accompanied by relations and friends who assisted in an unofficial capacity. Sabinus was senior to Vespasian and more advanced in his career at this stage

18. A. R. Burn, 'The Battle of the Medway, AD 43', *History*, 39 (1953), 105–15

19. Professor Birley informs us that Geta may have had six years seniority over Vespasian

20. *Numismatic Chronicle*, 6th Ser., 19 (1959), 17

21. *Britannia*, 1 (1970), 304

22. Sir Cyril Fox, *A Find of the Early Iron Age from Llyn Cerrig Bach, Anglesey* (1946)

23. R. C. Collingwood, *Roman Britain and the English Settlements* (1937), 85

24. Suetonius, *Galba*, 7

25. Suetonius, *Claudius*, 17

26. Suetonius, *Vespasian*, 4

27. Dio Cassius, lx, 21; Suetonius, *Galba*, 17 and 21; Josephus, *Bell. Jud.*, iii, 4

28. M. P. Charlesworth in *Cambridge Ancient History*, x, 699

29. '*Triumphavitque maximo apparatu*', Suetonius, *Claudius*, 17

30. *C.I.L.*, iii, x, 6809 ( = Dessau, *I.L.S.*, 2696)

31. Riese, *Anthologia Latina*, i, pp 419–26

32. For a full discussion see D. R. Dudley, 'The Celebration of Claudius' British Victories', *Birmingham Historical Journal*, 7, Pt 1 (1959), 1–17

33. F. Castagnoli, *Bulletin della Commissione Archaeologica del Governatoro di Roma*, 70 (1942), 74

CHAPTER 4

1. Tacitus, *Agricola*, 14

2. *Britannia*, 3 (1972), 149–63

3. Suetonius, *Vespasian*, 4. The idea put about later by the panegyrists of Vespasian that his conquests extended to Caledonia can hardly be taken at their face value (*J.R.S.*, 40 (1950), 41–42)

4. There remains the possibility that the Romans may have been mistaken in identifying two sections of the Durotriges as two separate tribes. It has been suggested by Mr C. E. Stevens that

there were two distinct administrative centres of the *civitas*, one at Dorchester and the other at Ilchester (*Proc. Somerset Arch. and N.H. Soc.*, 96 (1951), 188–92) which may have been the successors of the two great hill-forts of Maiden Castle (the Dunium of Ptolemy) and Ham Hill

5. Dorothy M. Liddell, 'Report on the Excavations at Hembury Fort', *Proc. Devon Arch. Expl. Soc.*, 2 (1935), 135–75

6. Reverend H. G. Tomkins, *Worlebury, An Ancient Stronghold in the County of Somerset*, 1866

7. *Arch.*, 14 (1803), 90–3. The collection is now in the British Museum

8. D. F. Allen, 'The Origins of Coinage in Britain: A Reappraisal', *Problems of the Iron Age in Southern Britain*, 97–308

9. Professor C. F. C. Hawkes, in *Bagendon* (1961), 46 ff

10. R. E. M. Wheeler, *Maiden Castle, Dorset* (1943)

11. Published like *Maiden Castle* as a Research Report of the Society of Antiquaries, London

12. *Problems of the Iron Age in Southern Britain*, edited by S. S. Frere, 88–90)

13. J. Brailsford, 'Early Iron Age "C" in Wessex', *Proc. Prehist. Soc.*, 24 (1958), 101–19

14. This is an over-brief summary of Mr D. F. Allen's conclusions in 'The Origins of Coinage in Britain: A Reappraisal', *Problems of the Iron Age in Southern Britain*. His Gallo-Belgic 'C' coinage was introduced into Britain from the south coast and copies of this, his British 'A' and 'B' became the progenitors of the Durotrigian types

15. These two small silver coins, Mack 371 and 372, found near Portsmouth and at Hod Hill respectively, are quite unlike any Durotrigian types and are closer in style to the Catuvellaunian issues. It has even been suggested that they may have stood for *Cogidubnus Rex Atrebatorum et Britannorum* (A. L. F. Rivet, *Town and Country in Roman Britain* (1958), 159), but this is rather fanciful and it is unlikely that Cogidubnus would have been allowed to mint his own coins after AD 43

16. Mr D. F. Allen's map in the Introduction to the OS *Map of the Iron Age of Southern Britain* (1962)

17. Tacitus, *Annals*, ii, 20

18. Sir Ian Richmond, *Hod Hill*, ii, 1968

19. Leslie Alcock, *By South Cadbury is that Camelot*, 1972

20. The original report was given in the *Proc. Soc. Ant.*, 4 (1856–9), but a reappraisal by Colin A. Gresham appeared in *Arch. J.*, 96 (1939), 114–31

21. Kathleen M. Kenyon, 'Excavations at Sutton Walls, Herefordshire, 1948–1951', *Arch. J.*, 110 (1953), 66–83. The evidence of decapitation here suggests that some of these victims had been executed

22. *V.C.H., Somerset*, I, p 295; *Proc. Somerset Arch. and N.H. Soc.*, 53 (1907), 181; 60 (1923), 49–53; 70 (1924), 104; 72 (1926), etc

23. J. A. Steers, *The Coastline of England and Wales* (1946)

24. I. D. Margary, *Roman Sussex* (1951), Pl 10. This 'Jockey cap' type of helmet was being replaced about this time by a different type with better neck protection. Helmets similar to that at Lewes are a sure sign of Claudian military activity

25. Now in the Ashmolean Museum, Oxford; formerly in the Medhurst Collection, *Gents. Mag.* (July, 1886); illustrated by E. T. Leeds in *Celtic Ornament* (1933), Fig 30b

26. Barry Cunliffe, *Excavations at Fishbourne*, 1971, Soc. of Antiquaries Research Report no 26. A shorter and more popular account is *Fishbourne, A Roman Palace and its Garden*, 1971

27. Alec Down and Margaret Rule, *Chichester Excavations*, i, 1970; further reports forthcoming; see also *Britannia*, 1 (1970), 302–3; 3 (1970), 350

28. *Proc. Devon Arch. Expl. Soc.*, 2 (1935), 200; 3 (1938), 67; 4 (1949), 20

29. *R.C.H.M., Dorset West*, i, 1952, 10–11

30. *Trans. Devonshire Association*, 62 (1931), 119–20; 91 (1959), 81

31. *Hod Hill*, i, *Antiquities from Hod Hill in the Durden Collection*, J. W. Brailsford, 1962

32. Op cit, note 19 above

33. The outstanding feature of the equipment from Ham Hill is the fine quality of the metalwork. The belt-plates and apron-mounts are probably legionary and so, it would appear, is much of the other equipment which is comparable only to similar items from known legionary fortresses (listed in *Arch. J.*, 115 (1958), 80–3)

34. Graham Webster, 'An Excavation at Nunnington Park near Wiveliscombe, Somerset', *Proc. Somerset Arch. and N.H. Soc.*, 103 (1959), 81–91

35. By Mr Norman Field, *Antiquity*, 42 (1968), 309–11; *see also* S. S. Frere, *Britannia*, 1961, 72–74

36. Lady Aileen Fox, *Roman Exeter* (1956).

37. *Proc. Devon Archaeol. Soc.*, 26 (1968), 1–20

38. *Proc. Dorset Arch. and N.H. Soc.*, 2 (1878), 109

39. The evidence advanced for military ditches at Camerton is insufficient, W. J. Wedlake, *Excavations at Camerton* (1958), 45

40. There is in the British Museum a legionary belt-plate said to have been found at Greenhill, Weymouth

41. The older idea that these burials were the result of a great battle of AD 845 between Saxons and Danes (A. Major, *Early Wars of Wessex*, 122) has been totally disproved. The excavator, Mr Philip Rahtz, has suggested that the Roman settlement nearby may have been the missing Iscalis of Ptolemy (OS *Map of Roman Britain*, Fig 1)

42. *J.R.S.*, 14 (1924), 232; *Trans. Bristol and Glos Arch. Soc.*, 61 (1939), 202; 65 (1944), 195; 66 (1945), 294; 68 (1949), 184; 71 (1954), 70; *Arch. J.*, 105 (1960), 89

43. *Roman Colchester*, 1958, Pl 1

44. The Thracian units in Britain at this stage present a problem. During the reign of Tiberius in AD 26, there had been serious trouble in Thrace when the soldiers heard reports that their units were to be broken up, mixed with those of other peoples and sent to distant provinces (*Annals*, iv, 46). Thrace itself was not made a province of the Empire until AD 46 but some arrangement must have been made earlier than this with one of the client kings for units to serve in the *auxilia* wherever they were needed

45. *V.C.H.*, *Roman Essex* (1963), 3

46. *Camulodunum*, 1947, Pls CII CIV; *Archaeol. J.*, 115 (1960), 75–78

47. *Trans. Essex Archaeol. Soc.*, 3rd ser. 2 (1968), 137–142; 3 (1971), 1–11; *J.R.S.*, 57 (1967), 189, 58 (1968), 196; *Britannia*, 3 (1972), 331; and unpublished results kindly supplied by the excavator, Mr R. Crummy

48. *V.C.H.*, *Roman Essex* (1963), 4

49. At Valkenburg, excavated by Professor Van Giffen, *J.R.S.*, 42 (1952), 129 and Pl xv. W. Glasbergen, *De Romeinse Castella te Valkenburg Z.H.*, 1972, 151

50. *J.R.S.*, 59 (1969), 223

51. *Britannia*, 3 (1972), 333
52. An assessment of the situation here is made difficult by the modern development which has only permitted small scale investigations over a large area (information kindly supplied by Mr Warwick Rodwell)
53. D. F. Allen, *The Coins of the Coritani* (1963)
54. Kathleen M. Kenyon, *Excavations at the Jewry Wall Site, Leicester*, 1948; Elizabeth Blank, *A Guide to Leicestershire Archaeology*, 1970, 13
55. Professor S. S. Frere, *Ant. J.*, 37 (1957), 4
56. *V.C.H., Herts*, IV, 158 and Pl 1. This helmet, which lacks its cheek-pieces, is now in Colchester Museum. There are actually three punched inscriptions done by three different owners, one of them beginning PP which stands for *primipilaris*, the chief centurion who commanded the first cohort, the crack unit in the legion
57. *Britannia*, 1 (1970), 288
58. *J.R.S.*, 55 (1965), 74–76 and Pl IX; 58 (1968), 189
59. Summaries in *J.R.S.* and *Britannia* and for a plan of the excavations up to 1970 see *Britannia*, 2 (1971), Fig 9, 265; and for a plan of the *principia*, *ibid*, 3 (1972), Fig 6, 321
60. Work is still continuing, information kindly supplied by Dr P. Wild and Mr G. Dannell
61. This fort was discovered from the air by O. G. S. Crawford as long ago as 1930 (*Antiquity*, 4 (1930), 274; 13 (1939), 455), but still remains to be investigated
62. *R.C.H.M., City of Cambridge* (1959), p xxxvi
63. There is an early military-type ditch below the civil settlement and a *dolabra* (a legionary pick-axe) has also been found; *Britannia*, 1 (1970), 287; 2 (1971), 264; and information kindly supplied by the excavator Mr H. M. Green
64. Tacitus, *Annals*, xii, 31. Accepting the brilliant textual emendation by Bradley *cunctaque cis Trisantonam et Sabrinam fluvios cohibere parat*
65. T. Davies Pryce, *Ant. J.*, 18 (1938), 29–48
66. The names of these Roman roads are of course of Saxon origin and thus have no association with their original purposes
67. *J.R.S.*, 55 (1965), 205; 56 (1966), 202. I am very grateful to Dr Stead for allowing me to see his report in typescript
68. *Lincs. Hist. and Archaeol.*, 1, No 1, Figs 4a and b
69. *R.I.B.*, 254, 255 and 267; 260 may be another, but it is im-

possible to reconstruct the full name from the surviving fragments

70. *V.C.H., Shrops.*, i, 1908, 244
71. I am grateful to Mr B. R. Hartley for information about this
72. *Arch.*, 58 (1903), 573 and Pl lv; this is now in Newark Museum
73. By Mr J. Wacher, *J.R.S.*, 54 (1964), 159, Fig 12, and Pl xii (1); 56 (1966), 203 and Fig 10; *Trans. Leics. Archaeol. and Hist. Soc.*, 45 for 1969–70, 7
74. By Dr Felix Oswald who worked almost single-handed on this site for many years. Several accounts of this work have been published by the University of Nottingham and in *J.R.S.*, 12 (1922), 249; 13 (1923), 114; 14 (1924), 255; 16 (1926), 36; 17 (1927), 195; 18 (1928), 199; 19 (1929), 193; 22 (1932), 206; 23 (1933), 196; 25 (1935), 77 and 210
75. Malcolm Todd, 'A Roman Settlement at Margidunum: The Excavations of 1966–8', *Trans. Thoroton Soc.*, 73 for 1969–70, 17–38
76. *Ibid*, 29
77. *V.C.H., Leics.*, i, 179–180; *Archaeol. J.*, 75 (1918), 25–27
78. Those few which have been used as evidence of early legionary dispositions are strays from later sites. The most difficult one to explain is the bath-house voussoir tile found near Helpstone, Northants, as the cover of a cremation burial and now in the Peterborough Museum. It is identical to tiles at York
79. E. Blank, *Ratae Coritanorum*, 1971, 9–12
80. *Itinerarium Curiosum*, ii, 1776, 96
81. *J.R.S.*, 55 (1965), 74–5, Fig 2
82. Some of these are now in the Margidunum collection in Nottingham University and others in the Castle Museum, Nottingham. A fine military mess-tin also came from this site, *Ant. J.*, 19 (1939), Pl 87, see also *E. Midlands Archaeol. Bull.*, No 8 (1965), 30
83. *J.R.S.*, 47 (1957), 210; (1965), Fig 12
84. *J.R.S.*, 56 (1956), 203; but it was cutting through earlier pits which contained Roman pottery (*J.R.S.*, 57 (1967), 182; 58 (1968), 184; 59 (1969), 214). Butt ends of the ditches found in 1969 may indicate the presence of a gate (*Britannia*, 1 (1970), 284
85. The result of this work has been published by Nottingham University in three reports, *The Roman Town and Villa at Great Casterton, Rutland* (1951, 1954, 1961)

86. Dr St Joseph had flown over this site in eight of the previous twelve years and nothing had been visible, then the drought of 1959 suddenly revealed the crop-marks of the fort, published in *Great Casterton III*, Pl ii

87. *The Roman Fort at Great Casterton, Rutland*, 1968

88. Carried out by Miss Elizabeth Blank on behalf of the Leicester City Museum (*Britannia*, 2 (1971), 258

89. Stamped 'MATVRVS', the maker, and now in Warwick Museum. It is very similar to others from Gloucester and Broxstowe. *Trans. Birmingham Archaeol. Soc.*, 81 for 1963–4 (1966), 143–4 and Pl 30

90. In Northampton and Kettering Museums respectively, there are also brooches of Hod Hill type from the latter

91. *Ant. J.*, 12 (1932), Pl xviii, No 8. The Roman road system suggests an early site west of the town, possibly at a place called Little Chesterton (*C.B.A. Archaeol. Group* 9, *Newsletter*, No 3 1973, 18–19)

92. In the Ashmolean Museum, Acc. No 1972, 2143. I am grateful to Mr C. Young for drawing my attention to this object

93. *Trans. Birmingham Arch. Soc.*, 66 for 1945 and 46 (1950), Pl xii, Fig 1, No 53

94. By Mr Steven Taylor in the Bleachfield Street area

95. *Trans. Birm. Archaeol. Soc.*, 83 (1969), 65–129; *Trans.* forthcoming

96. *J.R.S.*, 27 (1937), 168–169

97. *Trans. Birmingham Archaeol. Soc.*, 79 for 1961 and 61 (1964), 117–20; *J.R.S.*, 59 (1969), 217

98. By Mr Keith Scott who has kindly allowed me to anticipate his report

99. *Britannia*, 2 (1971), 263

100. *Reliquiae Britannicae Romanae*, ii; see also p 150

101. *Arch J.*, 115 (1958), Pl ix B

102. *R.I.B.*, No 121

103. His name was Dannicus of the Raucae, a tribe in Switzerland

104. Sextus Valerius Genialis, born in Frisia, now part of the Netherlands

105. It is unfortunate that this stone has become separated from its fellows and is now in Gloucester Museum

106. Most of these have been published, *Arch. J.*, 115 (1958), Figs 3, 71 and Pl xi B

107. *Ant. J.*, 42 (1962), 3–5; 43 (1963), 15–16; 45 (1965), 97–101. The situation here is complicated by the discovery of another military site at Watermoor on the south part of the town (*ibid*, 49 (1969), 222–25). Defences here, which cannot belong to those found by Mr Wacher, have not yet been firmly dated and the relationship between the two sites remains to be established

108. Neronian pottery has been found in excavations (*Britannia*, 1 (1970), 300)

109. There is part of a Flavian building inscription (*R.I.B.*, 172) and one of the men who died there was a soldier of the IInd *Adiutrix* (*R.I.B.*, 157), which was in Britain from only AD 71 to 86

110. *R.I.B.*, No 159; see also Barry Cunliffe, *Roman Bath*, 1969, 2

111. *J.R.S.*, 59 (1969), 227; *Trans. Bristol and Glos. Archaeol. Soc.*, 92 (1973), 60–91

112. This remarkable site was later developed into a religious centre, but there is a baldric loop from it in the Devizes Museum (*Wilts. Archael. Mag.*, 65B (1970), 195–8), and the presence of a fort suggested, but not on secure evidence (*J.R.S.*, 59 (1969), 229)

113. *Archaeologia*, 57 (1891), 244–5

114. *Archaeologia*, 102 (1969), Fig 5

115. *Britannia*, 1 (1970), 183, fn 26

116. *Archaeol J.*, 115 (1960), 84–7

117. Dio, lxi, 30

118. Suetonius, *Claudius*, 24

119. Part of one of the large wheels used in lifting the water out of one of the Spanish mines can be seen in the Greek and Roman Life Gallery at the British Museum

120. Silver was extracted from galena, an ore which is mostly lead compounds; the lead pigs are thus the waste products although the metal was widely used. This particular pig was found near Wookey Hole at Charterhouse as long ago as about 1540 and although lost, its inscription was recorded

121. *J.R.S.*, 58 (1968), 198

CHAPTER 5

1. Tacitus, *Annals*, xii, 31–40
2. E. M. Clifford, *Bagendon, A Belgic Oppidum* (1961), 155
3. J. E. Lloyd, *Owen Glendower* (1931), 93–5
4. It must be emphasized that the chronology of the events to be described is tentative. Tacitus provides two fixed points; the arrival of Ostorius Scapula in the autumn of AD 47 and the surrender of Caratacus '*nono post anno quam bellum in Britannia coeptum*', ie in AD 51. The sequence of events is certain, the problem is to try to determine which campaigns were undertaken in each summer. The dating we put forward seems to us reasonable, but we do not claim that it is certain
5. *Trans. Birmingham Arch. Soc.*, 58 for 1934 (1937), 68–83; 72 for 1954 (1956), 1–4. Excavations were carried out in 1968–69 by Mr Trevor Rowley (*Britannia*, 2 (1971) 263)
6. *William Salt Arch. Soc.*, for 1927 (1929), 185; *J.R.S.*, 19 (1929), 194
7. This was first noted by Dr St Joseph and considered to be a marching camp, *J.R.S.*, 48 (1958), 95; 53 (1963), Pl x, 3
8. *N. Staffs Field Club* (1912), 139
9. *Trans. Birmingham Arch. Soc.*, 74 for 1956 (1958), 12–25. This bath-house is now under Ministry of Public Building and Works guardianship
10. *J.R.S.*, 43 (1953), 83
11. *Trans. Birmingham Arch. Soc.*, 75 for 1957 (1959), 24–9; and report forthcoming
12. *Trans. Birmingham Arch. Soc.*, 79 for 1960–61 (1964), 11–23; *Lichfield and S. Staffs Arch. Soc.*, 5 (1964), 1–50; 8 for 1966–7 (1968), 1–38
13. *Trans. Birmingham Arch. Soc.*, 69 for 1951 (1953), 50–6
14. *Trans. Birmingham Arch. Soc.*, 73 for 1955 (1956), 100–8; *J.R.S.*, 43 (1953), 83–4; 48 (1958), 94
15. D. R. Dudley and Graham Webster, *The Rebellion of Boudicca* (1962), 109; for yet another fort see *J.R.S.*, 55 (1965), 76 and Fig 3
16. *J.R.S.*, 55 (1965), 76–7
17. *J.R.S.*, 59 (1969), 105
18. All these are in the Rowley House Museum, Shrewsbury; for

full details see *V.C.H., Shrops*, I, 244–6 and *R.I.B.*, 291–4 and 296

19. *Trans. Birmingham Arch. Soc.*, 69 for 1951 (1953), 54 and Fig 2; *J.R.S.*, 43 (1953), 84; 48 (1958), 95 and Pl xiii; a rather better photograph by Mr Arnold Baker has been published in *The Rebellion of Boudicca*, Pl xii

20. *Trans. Shropshire Archaeol. Soc.*, 59 (1972), 28

21. *J.R.S.*, 45 (1955), 88 and Pl xix; see also a possible extension of the system, *Trans. Shropshire Archaeol. Soc.*, 59 (1972), 26 and Fig 8

22. In the interim reports in *Ant. J.*, 1956–62

23. The characteristics of the three phases now established are: 1. trenches filled with clean sand showing buildings erected on sterile ground; 2. trenches filled with sand but also with pieces of clay and charcoal showing that timber buildings with clay walls had been built; and 3. wide trenches where the final phase building had been grubbed out by the demolition parties. The evidence from the baths has been confirmed by a section through the Roman street north of this building. Three periods of timber buildings have been found to underlie the first street, showing that the timber phases definitely preceded the setting out of the street plan; *Trans. Shropshire Archaeol. Soc.*, 59 (1972), 15–23

24. *Trans. Worcs. Archaeol Soc.*, 3rd ser., 2 for 1968–9 (1970), 13–16

25. *Trans. Birmingham Arch. Soc.*, 42 for 1938 (1943), 27–31

26. *Trans. Worcs Arch. Soc.*, 39 for 1962 (1963), 55–8

27. Summarized by Mr George Boon in *Monmouth Antiquary*, 1.2 (1962), 28–33 and an early samian bowl from Caerleon, 2.1 (1965), 42–51; *The Roman Frontier in Wales*, 1969, ed. by Michael G. Jarrett, 116–18; see also *Britannia*, 1 (1970), 273; 2 (1971), 246–7; 3 (1972), 302

28. *The Roman Frontier in Wales*, 2nd ed., 1969, 46; military objects of first-century date have also been found and I am grateful to Mr P. Ashmore for drawings

29. *Ibid*, 77–80

30. *J.R.S.*, 51 (1961), 125–6; S. S. Frere, *Britannia*, 1969, 84; *The Roman Frontier in Wales*, 2nd ed., 81

31. Listed in *Archaeol. J.*, 115 (1960), Nos 131–133, p 83

32. *Trans. Woolhope Club*, 39 (1968), 237

33. *J.R.S.*, 51 (1961), 125; 55 (1965), 85

34. 12 British and Roman Republican and 2 Claudian copies up to 1924

35. *Trans. Woolhope Club*, 40 (1970), 45–6

36. *Trans. Shropshire Archaeol. Soc.*, 58 (1967), 8–18

37. Information kindly supplied by the excavator. The presence of *Legio* XX in Gloucester is known from a lost tombstone (*R.I.B.*, No 122)

38. This takes the sequence of events beyond the scope of this book. *Legio* XIV was withdrawn from Britain by Nero in 66 and was replaced at Wroxeter by *Legio* XX. The vacancy at Gloucester was filled by *Legio* II *Aug*, but on a new site below the later *colonia*

39. *J.R.S.*, 43 (1953), 85, 48 (1958), 95; *Trans. Shropshire Archaeol. Soc.*, 57 (1966), 197; 58 for 1967–8 (1969), 195–6

40. *J.R.S.*, 51 (1961), 125; 55 (1965), 85

41. *J.R.S.*, 59 (1969), 120 and Fig 6

42. *J.R.S.*, 55 (1965), 85

43. J. K. S. St Joseph, 'Aerial Reconnaissance in Wales', *Antiquity* 35 (1961), 269; *The Roman Frontier in Wales*, 2nd ed, 1969, 123–6

44. *Guide to the Collection illustrating the Prehistory of Wales*, 1939, 119 and Pl IX, No 463

45. Cf. Tacitus, *Agricola*, 25, where Agricola learns from Caledonian prisoners of the alarm caused by the appearance of the Roman Fleet off the coast of Scotland

46. *Proc. Devon Archaeol. Explor. Soc.*, No 24, 1966

47. *Britannia*, 3 (1972), 344–5

48. *Cathedral Close Excavations*, Museum Publications No 67; Lady Aileen Fox has suggested to me that the timber building she published in *Roman Exeter*, 1952 (Fig 3) could have been a tribune's house on the *via principalis*

49. *J.R.S.*, 48 (1958), 98

50. *Britannia*, 3 (1972), 56–111

51. *Proc. Dorset Archaeol. and N.H. Soc.*, 82 (1961), 88–108; 86 (1965), 135–49; and report forthcoming

52. Tacitus, *Annals*, xii, 33, 'Set tum astu locorum fraude prior, vi militum inferior . . .'

53. *Antiquity*, 35 (1961), 270

54. *Roman Frontier in Wales*, 2nd ed, 1969, 66–70; *J.R.S.*, 59 (1969), 121–2

55. Tacitus, *Annals*, xii, 34–5
56. Tacitus, *Histories*, iv, 23; v, 16
57. Tacitus, *Agricola*, 37; *Annals*, xiv, 37
58. Tacitus, *Histories*, iv, 71
59. Tacitus, *Annals*, xiv, 36–8, describes the review, the speech of Caratacus, and the special session of the Senate
60. Zonaras, ii, 7
61. Syphax, Livy, xxx, 13; Perseus, Livy, xlv, 7–8; Plutarch, *Aemilius Paullus*, 26

CHAPTER 6

1. *Annals*, xii, 39–40
2. See Ref. No 24, chap. 5 and Dr Jarrett's 'Early Roman Campaigns in Wales', *Arch. J.*, 121 (1965), 13–39
3. Large temporary camps are known at Blaen Cwm Bach and Twyn-y-Briddallt (Glamorganshire), but these hardly qualify for the Tacitean word *praesidia* and probably fit better into a later context
4. Tacitus, *Annals*, iv, 23
5. '...ut quondam Sugambri excisi aut in Gallias traiecti forent, ita Silurum nomen penitus extinguendum.' *Annals*, xii, 39
6. '...ac praecipua Silurum pervicacia, quos accendebat vulgata imperatoris vox....' *id. ib.*
7. Eg in geology, Silurian limestone; in literature, the Silurist poets, etc
8. Quintilian, *Institutio Oratoria*, vi, 3, 68
9. On Manlius Valens see Dio, lxvii, 14, 5
10. '...et auxerat potentiam, postquam capto per dolum rege Carataco instruxisse triumphum Claudii Caesaris videbatur.' Tacitus, *Histories*, iii, 45
11. '...sed post captum Caratacum praecipuus scientia rei militaris Venutius....' Tacitus, *Annals*, xii, 40
12. For Stanwick see R. E. M. Wheeler, *The Stanwick Fortifications* (Society of Antiquaries Research Report, xvii), 1954
13. 'valida et lecta armis inventus regnum eius invadunt...' *id. ib.*
14. Text and translation of selected passages of *Y Gododdin*, the poem in which this exploit is recorded, may be found in *The Burning Tree* by Gwyn Williams (1956), 22 f

15. His full names were Quintus Petilius Cerealis Caesius Rufus. We owe this information to Dr Anthony Birley

16. '(*Venutius*) *quisuper insitam ferociam et Romani nominis odium propriis in Cartimanduam reginam stimulis accendebatur.*' Tacitus, *Histories*, iii, 45

17. '... *mox Didius Gallus parta a prioribus continuit, paucis admodum castellis in ulteriora promotis, per quae fama aucti officii quaereretur.*' Tacitus, *Agricola*, 14

18. At Strutt's Park on the other side of the river to that of the later fort – *Britannia*, 2 (1971), 256; *Derbyshire Archaeol. J.*, 90 (1970), 22–30

19. See V.C.H. *City of York*, 322

20. For Little Chester see Graham Webster in *Archaeological Journal*, 115 (1958), 63; for Templeborough see John Clarke in *Roman and Native in North Britain*, ed I. A. Richmond (1958), 36; and one might also add Newton Kyme, *J.R.S.*, 43 (1953), 87–8, Pl xi, 1; 45 (1955), 82, and 55 (1965), 77–8, Fig 2

21. *J.R.S.*, 59 (1969), 103 and Pl ii (1)

22. J. Wacher, *Excavations at Brough-on-Humber 1958–1961*, 1959, 5–8

23. *J.R.S.*, 55 (1965), 75 and Pl x; 59 (1969), 104

24. *Britannia*, 1967, 70–71

25. The only recorded find from Newton on Trent is a coin of 106 BC (*Lincs. Archaeol. and Hist.*, 1, No 1, 38) which may suggest a Claudio-Neronian date, since these early Republican coins are rare on later sites or it could be a stray

26. *J.R.S.*, 59 (1969), 105

27. For his epitaph (now in the Museo Romano at Rome) see *C.I.L.*, vi, 13272 and *L'Année Epigraphique*, 1953, nr 253. His significance is discussed by E. R. Birley, *Britain and the Roman Army* (1953), 1–9

# Index

(The numerals in **bold** type denote plate numbers)

If you have enjoyed this PAN
Book, you may like to choose
your next book from the titles
listed on the following pages.

*Leonard Cottrell*

THE GREAT INVASION                    30p

D-DAY AD43 – the beginning of the great
invasion. Four tough Roman legions – 50,000
men grouped in three divisions – began landing under the white cliffs of Dover. Infantry,
cavalry and engineers, supply troops in support, poured on to the Kent beaches while
the grim Britons faded into their swamp and
forest defence lines . . .

This evocative reconstruction brings to life
the armies who fought in the bitter forty-
year campaign. The soldiers and their equipment, their commanders and their plans, the
battles that were fought and won all provide
fascinating parallels with modern warfare.

This exciting book tells what the Romans
found here and why they came.

'So informs his narrative with insight into
common man that you almost smell the sweat
of fear . . .' – WESTERN MAIL

*Leonard Cottrell*

ENEMY OF ROME                                    40p

In May, 218 B.C., Hannibal of Carthage set
out from Spain with over 100,000 troops.

His destination – Rome
His aim – the destruction of its great Empire.

So began an immortal campaign that lasted
sixteen fierce and bloody years and revealed
Hannibal as an inspired military genius. His
concept of strategy was daring and revolu-
tionary, involving the use of elephants, new
tactics and novel means of warfare.

Through France, Italy and Africa his battles
resounded to the clash of personalities and
intrigue, culminating in a battle of giants
which was to decide the fate of European
civilization.

'Reads like a brilliant dispatch from a war
correspondent attached to Hannibal's army'

*Leonard Cottrell*

**BULL OF MINOS** 30p

The thrilling story of the great archaeological discoveries in Crete and the Greek mainland, made by Heinrich Schliemann and Sir Arthur Evans. These two men fired by the same enthusiasm recreated a civilization which showed that when Homer sang of Achilles, Agamemnon and the Trojan War, he sang of kings and heroes who really lived.

'Archaeology made live and interesting'
— ILLUSTRATED LONDON NEWS